CORN WOMAN SINGS

CORN WOMAN SINGS

A MEDICINE WOMAN'S DREAM MAP

Eleanor Barrón Druckrey, Ph.D.

iUniverse, Inc.
New York Bloomington Shanghai

CORN WOMAN SINGS
A MEDICINE WOMAN'S DREAM MAP

iUniverse books may be ordered through booksellers or by contacting:

iUniverse
1663 Liberty Drive
Bloomington, IN 47403
www.iuniverse.com
1-800-Authors (1-800-288-4677)

Because of the dynamic nature of the Internet, any Web addresses or links contained in this book may have changed since publication and may no longer be valid.

The views expressed in this work are solely those of the author and do not necessarily reflect the views of the publisher, and the publisher hereby disclaims any responsibility for them.

ISBN: 978-0-595-46343-5 (pbk)
ISBN: 978-0-595-70534-4 (cloth)
ISBN: 978-0-595-90638-3 (ebk)

Printed in the United States of America

In Memory of

John Christopher Barrón
and
Claudette Peculik Whitesides

Contents

Foreword, by Yvette G. Flores, Ph.D. xi

Acknowledgments xiii

Author's Notes xv

Introduction...xxi

Chapter 1:   Life Is the Dream.. 1

Chapter 2:   Naming It: Before Dawn 15

Chapter 3:   The World of the Dreamer...................................... 24

Chapter 4:   Remembering: Dreaming Is Reality...................... 34

Chapter 5:   Encounters with Spirit Beings: Shift in Paradigm 47

Chapter 6:   Destiny Beckons 58

Chapter 7:   Sacred Gifts 70

Chapter 8:   Nature's Aliveness... 82

Chapter 9:   Duality 93

Chapter 10: Corn Woman Sings: Initiation Completed............. 107

Chapter 11: Conclusion 125

Epilogue.. 131

Endnotes... 135

References 141

Index... 145

Foreword

La ante palabra, the word that goes before the story, the foreword to any book is designed to guide the reader, to contextualize the work, and to situate the author. "Corn Woman Sings: A Medicine Woman's Dream Map" has been a labor of love for its author, who literally dreamed her awakening into health and wholeness. To introduce this work and the author is an honor, to contextualize it is a challenge; for to do the dream map justice, one has to understand the history of indigenous people of this continent.

Dr. Barrón Druckrey presents the most salient historical facts in a concise and engaging manner. Indeed, to journey through the dream map places the reader *in* the historical moment where dreamers had to go underground and their healing traditions veiled in order to survive the ravages of the Conquest. To uncover the dream map allows the reader to understand the cultural legacies of contemporary Chicanas, Chicanos, Latinas, Latinos and Native American people.

As the reader follows the dream map, she or he is invited to journey within the self and beyond the limits of everyday consciousness. This is a path Dr. Barrón Druckrey followed herself. From migrant family origins, Dr. Barrón Druckrey's life parallels that of ancient dreamers — marginalized as a woman of color, as a child of migrant workers, as an intelligent girl within a social context that found smart girls of color a threat, she found transformation and healing within the messages of her dreams. Dr. Barrón Druckrey survived in the best sense of the word, largely through her dream work. Her encounters with Corn Woman return her own healing powers. In her own words, "On our way to hear Corn Woman's song, we are guided toward transformation, our most essential reason for dreaming." Through an analysis of decades of dreams, Dr. Barrón Druckrey uncovers the hidden meanings of her grandmother's stories, her parents' distress, her own vulnerability to illness of body and spirit. Within her dreams she finds the road home, to wholeness, to acceptance of her multiple identities, and her role as a contemporary healer. To contextualize the dreams, she pursues the study of ancient knowledge, from Aztec and Mayan codices to North American First Nation writings. Her dreams guide her to the study of healing and the practice of healing arts, and ultimately her dreams lead her to the writing of this map.

As the 5th Sun, the Sun of Movement according to the Aztecs, reaches its final cycle, indigenous nations await a new age of transformation. During the Fifth Sun, social movements and demands for justice, upheavals, wars and manmade disasters prevailed. Mother Earth trembled and wept and reminded us all of the frailty and folly of many humans. Alongside these *movimientos* came also the resurgence of *indigenismo* and the (re)awakening of consciousness. Those who had the gift of seeing multiple dimensions and who listened to the messages in their dreams began to prepare for the changes to come.

Dr. Barrón Druckrey offers us, through her dream map, a path towards personal transformation in anticipation of the Sixth Sun, the age of enlightenment. She lovingly invites us to find our own way home within our dreams. It is indeed wise to listen and acquiesce when spirit calls.

Yvette G. Flores, Ph.D.
Berkeley, Ca

Acknowledgments

Success of this ten-year project is due to the encouragement and cheering on by many of my family, friends, readers, colleagues, other researchers, dreamers, the Four Directions, as well as helpful spirits from other dimensions. The support has been bountiful.

I will begin by expressing my gratitude to the editors who have graciously extended their assistance and provided valuable feedback and direction. To John Kriebel, for his gentle spiritual nature and dedication; to Netty Kahan, for her patience and attention to detail, a gift especially required for this project; to David Reichard, for his generous offer of help; and to Charles Durham of IUniverse for his invaluable assistance in editing the final drafts of the manuscript.

A special acknowledgment and note of appreciation goes to Dr. Yvette Flores, of the University of California, Davis, without whose assistance the shape and form of *Corn Woman Sings* would not have taken its present form. I am grateful for her spiritual guidance and support, and for the gift of her historical, literary, sociopolitical, anthropological, and psychological knowledge that filled and rounded out the corners of the story. I will always remember that she patiently gave of her time, even when the images were only disconnected, fragmented pieces of dreamscape that could have easily been overlooked and undervalued. She accepted the challenge of editing the original manuscript when there was no story, and then she took me by the hand as I wrote the dissertation for my doctorate in clinical psychology. To Dr. Flores, I am deeply indebted.

A word of thanks also goes to Dr. Jill Gover for her support and guidance in the creative unfolding of the possibilities this story presented.

To Dr. Luca DiDonna, for the vision and holding the thought, thank you.

To the readers who painstakingly read the manuscript and gave feedback, help, and encouragement: my friend Susan Raddelt; Dr. Susan Banks, at the University of Washington; Betty Rothenberger, MS, of the Jean Dixon Mystery School; and Caroline Van Tuyll of the Nyingma Institute.

For the numerous discussions on spirituality, consciousness, and awareness that assisted me in learning to trust my inner guidance, I wish to thank my friends and sisters in the spirit: Kathleen M. Baca, medicine woman and helper of the disenfranchised; Diana Marto, whose art inspires and manifests the feminine face of God; and Yana Womack, PhD, also for her work on dreaming in the Buddhist tradition; Br. Camilo Chavez, PhD, of St. Mary's College, Fr. William Myers, and Rev. Dr. Ernest White.

To my brothers, Juan de Dios Barrón and José Barrón, who have always supported and believed in me; and to my sister-in-law Angelina Miranda Barrón for her support and encouragement. To my husband's family, the Druckreys, and all my wonderful nieces and nephews who have anxiously waited for this completion.

To my friend Gary Politzer—artist, dreamer, medicine man—who generously offered to support this endeavor from the beginning of the writing, developed the website for it, and shot the photos for the cover. For his open heart, friendship, and technological support, I am deeply grateful.

To my husband Randall Druckrey—who many evenings brought me food, took me to dinner, distracted me when I needed it, made me laugh when the end of the world seemed near—and for his guidance and spiritual insights throughout this time, my deep love and appreciation.

And, lastly, but ever foremost, to my deceased parents who taught me to dream, to my grandparents and a long line of dreamers, to our Great Mother, the Spirit of Corn Woman, to the Four Directions, and to the spirits from other dimensions who revealed themselves and counseled me, I give thanks for the challenge you set before me. Thank you for this magnificent gift!

Author's Notes

I am a Chicana dreamer. My story begins in 1967, when a voice startled me out of my sleep, *"Do you want to know?"* In the early hours of the morning, this voice was inviting me on a journey of exploration through the multilevels of reality. Sitting up quickly, I pulled my blue blanket around myself to keep warm. Through the gap in the curtains, the lights of San Francisco streaming in, I could see a dark face with a mustache, kissing-distance from mine. "Do you want to know?" he repeated in a husky voice. Such appearances were common in my culture, and I had been dabbling in metaphysical realms for years, but being asked such a question was different, rankling, and disconcerting. I was not ready. I murmured back an unequivocal, no, and for ten years, closed myself off to such investigations. I was twenty-three years old.

Stalked and harassed by spirits that followed me during the day, and at night stepped closer—gently putting pressure on my back and my stomach, teasing, cajoling—I made a decision: to become conscious. I did not have a name for it then. I simply wanted to find reality, and to use my time on Earth as efficiently as possible.

I began practicing yoga. I did not want to reach the age of sixty with stiff muscles and creaky bones, and I wanted to make resilience my friend.

I also began keeping a dream journal. It seemed foolish to me not to know where or how I was spending one-third of my life. If at the end of the day, I could remember what I had eaten for breakfast, then I should be able to remember at the end of the night what I had done, seen, and felt. Amnesia of my nighttime activities while my body lay unconscious seemed absurd. When I first began the journal, disconnected random images appeared—a knife, a mysterious figure in dark shadows—and feelings of terror and rage. But at some definite point, I discerned a storyline unfolding.

As the strand of dreams took increasing shape and form, a dream of initiation came to me, and I entered it into a special journal. Otherwise, it would have gone unrecognized as the beginning of a tapestry of forays into other worlds and meetings with spirit beings. Without my realizing it, with the initiation dream I had so carefully tucked away, a lifetime of training emerged.

Cosmic Mother of the Americas

Several years passed before I recognized that the weaving of my sleeping and waking lives was creating an array of relationships and inexplicable places. A feminine figure appeared regularly. At first, I mention her in the journals as "an old Indian woman" who befriended and spoke to me in Spanish. How different it was—hearing Spanish again. She invited herself on the journey with me. *"Voy contigo?"* ("Shall I join you?") She asked. Within a heartbeat, I answered, *"Sí, cómo no."* ("Yes, of course.")

Little did I know that with her dazzling smile and dancing eyes, she would trick me into dreaming. Grandmother's teachings led me to search out and remember the noble knowledge and traditions that had fallen into disuse in my culture. Through her coaching, I found a labyrinth that spiraled me upward into the vastness of the universe where we had once flourished, and I entered the realm where gods drink the nectar of truth and vanish into other realities. I found the place where Corn Woman sings and summons us to remember her. Though the road was crooked, filled with potholes, boulders, and other obstructions, she finally emerged as the *Cosmic Mother of the Americas*.

The Elders' Request

Between 1977 and 1993, a group of elders appeared to me about three times, each time in a sacred underground cave. I shakily responded to what I thought they were asking of me: that I string the dreams together and leave a body of work that would explain the broader reality known to the indigenous peoples of the Americas—dreamers, artists, musicians, dancers, and storytellers. After receiving this directive from the elders, I plowed through twenty-five years of dream journals, categorizing and looking for themes. From them, I developed a 435-page manuscript that I titled, *Corn Woman Sings: An Autobiography from the Fifth Dimension*, and which I sent out to seventy publishers, with no positive results. It was a good story, but the meaning was somehow lost or unclear.

Discouragement led me to dig deeper, and I decided to do a formal investigation of my book's problems. As a result, I began looking for a doctorate program with sufficient flexibility to allow me to use my own data for the necessary doctoral research.

I had accumulated hundreds of dreams. Out of thirty journals and three three-inch-thick typed binders, I chose two hundred dreams that I felt might be related to the worldview of the early Mesoamerican cultures. By the time I was ready to tackle the research, I had a rough idea which aspects of the Chicana and other indigenous culture dreams were linked with the psychological, anthropological, and cultural components. I was *completely* stunned when the Feminine came into view. I had no cultural reference that would help me put her into perspective.

To do the research, I needed fifty thousand dollars. I was ill and unemployed at the time. Looking for funding, I sent out another thirty proposals—and again, all the responses were negative. But destiny put me in touch with a woman who was to become a kindred spirit and sister. Through her network, the doors opened to an agency that funded the entire project.

My birthplace is Whittier, California. Both of my parents were from Mexico. My father was a musician, playing the guitar for the orchestra that performed on *la Calle Olvera* in Los Angeles. A visionary, he prepared us for the future by taking us out of rural Pico Rivera in 1945, to Stockton, California, where he could give us a home with sidewalks and schools nearby. My mother, who was the container of all those things necessary to meet our family's needs, spread her arms wide to take on the challenge of getting us educated. In 1945, she and my father strayed from their Catholic roots and joined a fundamentalist church.

My Family and I

My brothers and I graduated from California schools. But, what made our lives extraordinary—besides our parents' having fortified us each with a musical instrument—was that my father worked for Western Pacific Railroad, giving us access to free travel by train on the American continents. I was nine when we began to take trips to Mexico City for our summer vacations. These journeys would take us through the vast expanse of the desert and red mesas of the Southwest, on through the rugged, lush green Sierra Madre of Central Mexico, where we stopped at every *ranchito*—those small clusters of dwellings in remote, isolated places—where local venders met us, selling their handmade artifacts: embroidered blue, white, and pink cotton blouses; wooden toys; pottery; and wonderful enchiladas with the sweetest, hottest mole I have ever tasted.

Five days of travel passed slowly, but when at last we rolled into Mexico City where my mother's family lived, our lives took on a new tenor and tempo. We picnicked in Chapultepec and visited the floating music and flowers in Xochimilco, museums, and went to *quinceañeras*—those wonderful debut parties given for fifteen-year-old young women.

The most magical part of traveling in Mexico was seeing the round, brown faces, dark eyes, and jet-black hair of the people. Seeing my family in the context of the Mexican culture added a new dimension to the texture of my North American life. The richest part was hearing stories about my family's past. My grandmother was a storyteller, and the private conversations I overheard between her and my mother placed me in a lineage of people whose destiny had already been lived out.

Home again, I noticed that the accoutrements of sidewalks, education, music, and culture came at great sacrifice to the family, and that we were all paying our dues. Summers, my brothers picked tomatoes, topped onions, and worked in the citrus groves of California. In the fall, my mother left home for two months working as a cook in a *bracero*—a Mexican laborer camp in the Stockton Delta. My father worked nights, and by day he helped her with the cleanup. Then, February through June, she returned.

I still remember with sadness the first time I was left with foster parents, a young couple from our church. I stood at the kitchen window as the shadow of night chased the sun and its radiant orange and purple light out of sight. I was six years old. "Two weeks," my mother had said. It seemed like an infinity in which I wondered if I would make it through that first night.

Over the following ten years, the disruption to our family played itself out in countless ways and times. This scene of parting and coming together again repeated itself in different houses, with different families, but with it, ever the same chilling feeling settled into my bones. I was like the goddess splitting my time between the upper- and underworlds six months at a time. With the passing of years, it seemed to me that my family grew accustomed to my absence, and that the gap that I had originally left was now covered over like ivy grows over a door that is no longer opened.

As I look back on my life, I can say that training for this task the elders assigned me began as a child. My father's morning conversations with my mother usually began with, "*Oye vieja, anoche soñé que ...*" "Last night I dreamed that ...," and he would launch into a dream story. In my father's love of dreams and Mexican music, and my mother's determination to keep our Mexican heritage vibrant, this dream map that I give you now was born. Destiny has provided me with a circuitous road. I've undergone the painful rounding off of sharp edges and corners of the ego and the psychological self that I once knew, to bring forth this gift. Whatever hardships or disappointments I have suffered on its behalf, I can now say that I did it gladly. The labor pains have been worth it because the value of the gifts I received have far outweighed the pain of the struggle.

This is Corn Woman's gift to us, and to the next seven generations.

Eleanor Barrón Druckrey, PhD
Tiburón, CA
May, 2007

Introduction

A Dream Map

If you have been stepping from rainbow to rainbow, flying over snow-covered mountain peaks, and walking rugged valleys with your head hung low, you will immediately intuit the winding course this dream map lays out. And, if you have heard stories or seen flashes of a phenomenal world beyond the world of your physical eyes, this map will open doors for you that will help you find your way to the Golden City, the glory of our cultural past. But most important, if you have been blessed with sacred gifts and need to understand the paradigm of your world, as you turn these pages that lead you into the haunts of the Old Dreamers, you will find familiar ground to help you manifest your own destiny. For the *curanderas*—the healers, the medicine women of the culture—and for mystics/artists everywhere, the door swings open for your grand return. *Bienvenida*, welcome home! Destiny waits for you to take your rightful place in history. Bring your medicine bundle and revitalize yourself in the fountains of old wisdom.

The mystical world of dreams impacts people of all walks of life, especially *curanderas*, artists, musicians, writers, educators, psychologists, storytellers, mystics, and theologians. No one is excluded from hearing the call of Spirit who appears in our dreaming. For all dreamers/artists/healers who have felt spiritually bereft and misunderstood in a world that values only the concrete, this dream map takes you by the hand to guide you home.

For the Chicana dreamer who seeks explanations for the snips and bits of stories she has heard of the great dreamers of the past, or who hungers for confirmation of something vague that she intuits, this dream map will bring instant recall to her genetic memory. She will remember the place before time where *La Virgen's* grandmother's grandmother's grandmother laid the platform for her life. Our past is magical, and we carry that magic and wonder within us.

Entering your dreams poses challenges, and this dream map will show you what you will need and what to do once you've entered through the golden gate. For instance, finding yourself face-to-face with a menacing spirit, you'll need to remember that energy and emotional states in your dreams require your undivided attention.

A menacing face does not necessarily indicate danger, and a split-second decision may facilitate your receiving a gift of power often hidden behind a ferocious facade. Also, while in other dimensions, you'll need to remember that spirit beings will be available to assist you in attaining your purpose in life. You will receive the gentle words of kindness and encouragement from our Great Mother, the Cosmic Mother of the Americas. For these reasons, breathing deeply when you're experiencing the profoundest of fears is very important. Knowing when to run and when to stay put are all part of the resources you will need once you've passed through the gates of dreaming.

Dreamers throughout the ages have traveled the byways of dreamtime and brought back nuggets of truth to the waking world. For nearly thirty years now, I have been recording my dreams. This is the story of how I came upon the treasures of the past and, in my dreamtime, was called by a group of elders to bring the old dream traditions back to *El Norte*—the Southwestern United States that was once northern Mexico—a region where they are long overdue and badly needed.

Ancient Dream Traditions

This dream map is based on the dream traditions of the Mesoamerican and North American dream cultures prior to the arrival of the Europeans. I will describe the process by which I connected the old dream traditions to my dream life and learned to interact with the Divine Mother and Father, and how I developed the ability to make conscientious decisions in the dream state. But the map's message is not about me, nor is it about any personal ownership I might have to it. This dream map urges us to embrace the noble teachings that inform us of the unity of all creation as the Old Dreamers of Mesoamerica and North America taught. On our way to hear Corn Woman's song, we are guided toward transformation, our most essential reason for dreaming.

My study, *The Contemporary Role of the Chicana Dreamer* (Barrón-Druckrey, 2001), examines the early American dream traditions, and in particular the Aztec and Maya. However, in this dream map, I focus on how dreaming today can be explored through the lenses of the Old Dreamers and how their worldview can assist the modern *curandera*, medicine woman, and mystic dreamer. I will briefly highlight only those details of my investigation that shed light on my story.

An interpretation of the religions, old values, and beliefs is necessary to bridge the gap between our modern thinking and the meaning implied in dream sequences. The role of the dreamer today is embedded in several key spiritual values and beliefs of the Maya, Aztec, and North American cultures as established by the Creation Stories. The Creation Stories are the accounts of the first Five Worlds as discussed in records left to us by the sages. The accounts were reconstructed from memory after the Spaniards destroyed and burned the ancient books. Here are highlights of the old worldview as they relate to this dream map:

- Before time and memory, there was only darkness, water, and the God of Duality, male and female; it was she who created the heavens and gave us corn—the spirit and light to sustain us; *Omecihuatl* is her Aztec name, *Xmucané* is her Mayan name. *Ometeotl* and *Xpiyacoc* are their masculine counterparts. Very importantly, these goddesses are represented in a variety of cultures throughout the Americas—their names corresponding to the culture and language in which they are found.[1] But today, the Chicana culture knows that *La Virgen de Guadalupe* derives from the compassionate goddess *Tonantzin* who was related to Omecihuatl and Xmucané.

- Because dreamers/priests were present at the time of creation, they were imbued with powers to transform, see, heal, make, and destroy events and matter. At the time of the arrival of the Spaniards in the Land of Mexica, a large group of sages known as the *Tlamitamines* existed, and they played a wide range of roles throughout the Aztec culture; they were statesmen, mystics, warriors, priests, educators, healers/psychologists, artisans, dancers, musicians, stone masons, jewelers, and more.

  As healers/psychologists, their role was to assist people in deciphering their destiny, and to "give a face and heart" to the seeker; but most important was their role to prepare the way for the future of the culture.[2] This point is the key that opens the door to understanding one's destiny and place in the universe. This theme is interwoven throughout this dream map.

- The God of Duality, a dual-gender god, known by many other names, determined the destiny of the people, and endowed them with gifts of power to live out their destiny.[3]

- Opposites in life represented the God of Duality, and transcendence was the ultimate goal.[4]

- The seat of reality was in the realm of dreams, which then established waking time as the dream.[5] The dream world was real, and the waking world was illusion.

- Time was imbued with the Divine.[6]

- Space was sacred and multidimensional. Travel between dimensions was possible and included communication with the departed[7] and spirit beings.

- Nature was a creation of the Divine and imbued with creative power of its own.[8]

- *Nagualismo*, transmutation (changing into other species) was possible.

The religions that developed around the spiritual teachings of the sages provided the political power necessary to perpetuate the culture. The Tlamitamines, the Old Dreamers, were believed to have significant powers that made them kin to the gods. They practiced their skills and traveled back and forth in time; they used the deeper levels of consciousness for healing and for helping people discover their destinies, understand reality, and find their places in the world. But it was because they dreamed and studied dreaming that they saw reality in its totality. They saw that everything in the universe was imbued with the power of creation, and they understood that they themselves had the tools, skills, and means to go deep into the complexities of the Divine.

The Tlamitamines went underground at the time of the Spanish conquest, because the conquest had made it unsafe to believe that an individual was endowed with special powers. When European culture and religion became the measure of true reality and the sacred, it labeled the philosophy of the Tlamitamines superstitious, dangerous, and a threat to the new order. Over time, it grew risky for traditional dreamers to have discourse on their practices and pass them on to the following generations—especially in plain view of the Catholic Church. But they had been forewarned; they had foreseen the demise of the culture long before the arrival of the Spaniards, and had prophesied that it would happen. They also prophesied that a resurgence of their culture would take place around the year 2011 CE.[9]

Pockets of the old cultures evolved in such a way that many of the old traditions are still intact today. However, here in *"El Norte,"* usually we only hear of these traditions and practices as *stories* in which truth and myth exist side-by-side, and no one understands their deeper purpose.[10],[11] Keep in mind that, although the Chicana culture of the United States has been twice colonized and that many sociopolitical and historical factors have impacted its development, its people are the result of an intermingling of the Spaniard and the Indian; we are the *Mestizo*. Although we have thrived and overcome substantial obstacles, we are bereft of our own essential ancient traditions.[12]

Dreaming is still important to us, but many have lost the knowledge regarding the roots and purposes of our dreams. As Mexican land was being changed into what we now think of as the Southwestern United States, many Chicana cultural values and traditions got blurred. Five hundred years have passed since the old teachings went underground, but now, fortunately, much of the information that was lost is now surfacing.

The Map

Here is what you will find in this dream map:

- Chapter 1. "Life Is the Dream" discusses preparation for starting a dream journal—an entering into a symbolic initiation—and what you may find as you search out the byways of deeper realities. The chapter highlights the unraveling of the dreamer's life simultaneously with the integration of her mind, body, and spirit. It gives guidelines for going inward and viewing life from the old worldview. The chapter examines the benefits of engaging with a spiritual community and with other sources of support. Visions can be very frightening, and we discuss the value of confronting the fear with breath awareness and other practices.

- Chapter 2. "Naming It: before Dawn" examines the sacred text, *The Popol Vuh,* which replaced *The Books of the Red and Black Ink* after the Spaniards destroyed them; and describes the history and religions of the Maya and Aztecs. Corn Woman's message of transformation derives from these legends that thus establish her as the Cosmic Mother of the Americas. The chapter briefly traces a history of goddesses from earlier cultures up to *La Virgen de Guadalupe,* the Virgin Mother of today's Catholic Church of Mexico. The chapter investigates transformation as seen through the themes of the God of Duality, fire, time and space, multidimensionality, and nagualismo.

- Chapter 3. "The World of the Dreamer" looks at the traditions of the early dreamers, sages, and philosophers known as Tlamitamines, and defines the old paradigm, which includes duality, time and space, nagualismo, and power. The Chapter also discusses the background of the split of the dream tradition after the Spanish invasion, and the tradition's influence in the reshaping of the Catholic Church in Mesoamerica. It tells how some of the Old Dreamers fled from positions of power into the shadows of the secret underground world, where they maintained their culture and prepared for the resurgence they anticipated 435 years from their own time. To illustrate similarities in paradigms, the chapter also discusses examples from North American dream traditions and concludes with an example of how communication occurs between dimensions and between spirit beings and humans.

- Chapter 4. "Remembering: Dreaming Is Reality" tells why developing powers of attention within the dream is crucial to discovering the path toward Corn Woman's message of transformation. This chapter defines the journey of the medicine woman and mystic, and tells of that early stage where we begin to pull back the curtain on reality. I cite examples from stories found in documents written at the time of the Spaniards, and dream journals that illustrate my parallel process.

- Chapter 5. "Encounters with Spirit Beings: Shift in Paradigm" explores the Mesoamerican world's perception of reality, including the interchange of humans with spirit beings. It examines examples of interchanges between spirit and human found in translations of old records, and my dream experiences with Grandmother. The chapter also talks about the feminine face of God as I began to perceive it.

- Chapter 6. "Destiny Beckons" considers how the dreamer's destiny is revealed, and that destiny's impact upon the life of the dreamer/*curandera*. Beliefs in destiny and fate are in direct opposition to Western thinking. Westerners find it difficult to accept that our inability to alter our destiny does not negate personal responsibility. For the dreamer, facing the creative power of the universe is daunting and treacherous, but doing so opens doors to sacred gifts that empower the dreamer to follow destiny's dictates. It also investigates the belief in destiny that is prevalent in the Chicana culture today in light of its origin in particular passages of the Creation Stories.

- Chapter 7. "Sacred Gifts" is the chapter in which I use the example of the life of Black Elk, a Lakota holy man of the nineteenth century to illustrate the role of sacred gifts in the healer's life. I discuss how these gifts are defined by destiny and how they manifest in the life of the modern-day dreamer/healer. The discussion includes the way these gifts are transmitted and the responsibility involved in accepting them. I give examples of the gifts I discovered as I worked in the field of death and dying, and tell of my struggles in living up to my responsibility for those gifts.

- Chapter 8. "Nature's Aliveness" explains the belief central in Native American religion that all nature is alive, and finds roots for the beliefs in the oneness of all creation. Passages from the Creation Stories are used to illustrate how the beliefs were perpetuated, and I also use examples from my dream journals to illustrate this reality in the modern-day dreamer's paradigm.

- Chapter 9. "Duality," delves into my experience of taking responsibility for my spiritual growth and the pitfalls and payoffs I encountered. The Old Dreamers believed that transcending duality was their single purpose for living. I use my dream journals to illustrate my own psychological homelessness and the way I dealt with it that facilitated my process of transformation. Facing this stage of initiation is a crucial opening for Corn Woman's message to surge through.

- Chapter 10. "Corn Woman Sings: Initiation Completed," reveals why and how the Old Dreamers saw the dream world as reality and waking as the dream. The Old Dreamers' journey to personal freedom could be translated into modern terms as *transformation* or *transcendence*. The dreamer—having gone through the arduous phases of integrating mind, body and spirit; deciphering his or her destiny, receiving a "face and heart," and going beyond duality—ultimately is brought face-to-face with Corn Woman's message and receives her blessing.

- Chapter 11. "Conclusion," is a wrap-up of the journey the dreamer travels, and translates these concepts into modern-day life.

- Epilogue. The epilogue tells, through dream and waking time, where I found my true home.

By drawing from the old dream traditions, the map leads you toward your personal transformation. It takes you through the process of coming to know why the Old Dreamers were seen as akin to gods, and how their lives evolved around this essential wisdom. It illustrates how you, as *curandera*/artist/writer/dancer, and the like, can decipher your understanding of reality and use the power that is your natural inheritance. You will come to see that you are made in the likeness of our Creatrix/Creator and, as a result, you will want to walk humbly upon the earth.

The Dreams

The dreams do not appear in chronological order; they are arranged in sequence of deepening awareness as my own process of integrating mind, body, and spirit unfolded. I attempt to keep a timeline to aid in understanding the sequence of dreams and events. The dreams are indented and italicized, and comments follow directly afterward.

My personal story, experience, and development are woven throughout this dream map, and delve into the effects of poverty and the Christian overlay upon my family. I explore the phenomenon of psychological homelessness within the Mexican American culture and my process of validating the spiritual truths, particularly about the Cosmic Mother, that were revealed to me.

In living your experience of this dream map, I encourage you to imagine yourself as my *comadre* or *compadre*—terms of endearment for the godparents of our children, literally, co-mother or co-father. Enter my home through the kitchen door to *platicar*—or chat. Over a cup of coffee, we can join in conversation about those crucial areas of life that arise so clearly in the early hours of the day. While we savor the coffee, we will pause and study the clouds passing in the sky, and reflect deeply. When destiny calls, it's wise to listen and acquiesce.

CHAPTER 1

▼

Life Is the Dream

I am not the first to dip her ladle into the Milky Way. As my dream journals mounted in number, I did not know what they symbolized. I was confused about many things that I was seeing: Grandmother, Corn Woman, a feminine god, spirit in nature. I stumbled and fell many times attempting to live up to the gifts I received. I had the feeling I was living in a house of mirrors, trying to find which was the reflection and which was the reality as I sought to decipher the meaning of the paradigm I had uncovered. I yearned to satisfy a need rumbling deep within my being, and looking to the stars felt like a logical source to turn to; because looking to the stars is a long-held tradition of my Mexican ancestors.

Though people of the Americas have not forgotten the Cosmic Mother, the Creatrix of our existence, we *have* forgotten that her power and wisdom reside within, and that she calls us yet to reclaim our wholeness and place in the universe. We have lost the meaning of the legends and stories and how they aid us in our modern-day lives. When I encountered Corn Woman in my dreams, I pondered the identity of the beautiful spirit who had touched my heart. I turned on my back the following morning to think on her, her name came to me in a sweet melody.

I had the dream in 1995, and it took eleven years to unravel the mystery of who she was and how she related to my cultural past. I studied history at the University of California at Berkeley because in my early adult years, I'd begun to suspect that something dreadful had occurred in my people's past. The answers I'd found only opened a mysterious box of more questions as I began my descent into time. Intimacy with my own people's culture evaded me.

The Call of Destiny

The gap widened as I came upon the paradigm that contradicted the religion of my youth. Imagine my amazement at finding the feminine face of God, where the Mother is as powerful as the Father of Western Christianity. In my fundamentalist Christian childhood, the message was that the native religions were, at best, heretical and demonic.

In an odd way, I've always felt that destiny beckoned me, and certainly, there have been many forces that catapulted my life in directions that brought me face-to-face with that destiny. It called most certainly when my three-year-old sister's death occurred on October 28, 1940, three years before I was born. Other challenges set my course as well, and without them, I venture to say that I wouldn't have hastened to my appointment with it.

But my sister's death set me in motion along the course that was to be mine—even before I was born. My parents had named her after a fair-skinned, green-eyed aunt on my father's side of the family, whose name was Leonor. *Leonorsita,* as they called my sister, was also fair-skinned and had light brown hair and eyes. She was a little princess born after two boys, and when she was three years old, she was suddenly taken ill with pneumonia. My parents' grief still remained unresolved when I was born on October 27, 1943—the third anniversary of my sister's death short by only one day—and they named me *Leonor* also. On my birth certificate, my name appears in English as Eleanor. I didn't like my name, because somehow it made me feel invisible, and it sounded too harsh in Spanish. Someone once called me *León,* lion, and that made me recoil from it even more. I'm brown-skinned, my eyes are black, and I once had a jet-black mane.

Even as a child, I knew something was off kilter, but could not name it. To compound the issue, my eldest brother John married an Eleanor whose birthday was October 26. I prayed to get my sister back, and I loved the idea. But it was disconcerting to be identified with three others who had the same name. Besides, the name never really became mine; in my family I was always called *Noni*, a nickname that is with me today. I felt displaced, and eventually I walked away from the family thinking I would leave the feelings of homelessness behind.

I open this dream map with these thoughts and feelings to let you know who I am. I have been an outsider since I was in my mother's womb. If you have picked up this book, you too have your reasons for it. Somewhere in the deepest part of your soul, you also long to find your way home. I am glad you are joining me on this path of self-discovery and truth. Destiny is calling.

The Dream Journey

The Mayan dreamers/healers, the Daykeepers of Guatemala, believe that the dream will struggle against the dreamer to be forgotten.[13] The process of pulling back the veil that separates the dream from the waking world is one of remembering either of the worlds in which you find yourself. Becoming awake *within the dream* and learning to dream *within the waking world* takes commitment, practice, and fierce determination. Dreams have a life and will of their own and being blessed with their abundance requires only the agility and tenderness it takes to trap a moonbeam.

If you decide to embark on this journey, the usual luggage will be unnecessary; your cell phone, even a compass will be superfluous. Instead, you will need sharpened senses, a pair of eyes that know, ears to witness silence, feet with wings, faith, courage, and an incredible amount of tenacity. Reality as you know it today will be blasted out from under you. Expect to be terrified, because you are about to step into infinity, where only your presence of mind counts. Many venture on this journey, and many get lost in space and time. There is a toll to pay, but the rewards you reap will ripple throughout this and many lifetimes to come.

On this fearless path of the dreamer, you will recover the brilliance that is normally beyond your reach and out of view: you've actually decided to become awake within *the great dream*. You will recognize that waking life *is* the dream; and dreaming is the time where real decisions are made, where the eyes witness the eternal light of life. In the beginning, assume that you, the dreamer, will encounter those places that one often ignores, that shake your senses and challenge your sanity. Welcome these moments as one would the warmth of a fire in the hearth after trudging through blasting and biting storms. Also assume that as you extend light into darkened caves that at first appear to be permanently stale and suffocating spaces, compassion awaits. I have found no place in my travels into other worlds where compassion is hidden from me or reserved only for those more deserving. Always trust your process and expect to be amazed, because you, a seeker, have entered into an initiation, and you are bound to confront the unknown with unplanned or unexpected reactions. Anything can be asked of you. Anything can happen—it is between you the dreamer and the Great Mystery.

So, you might wonder, why would I want to apply for this hazardous mission? I will tell you in just one word—awareness—an increase in your ability to understand the mysteries of the universe, attunement with the Divine, The Mother, and the powers of her medicine bundle: expanded consciousness, intuitive gifts necessary to accomplish those tasks destiny requires of you, wisdom, knowledge, and, best of all, transformation.

This chapter explains the primary task that will be yours in the early stages of dreaming. This task will, with time, branch out and grow into new stages. The integration of mind, body, and spirit is critical to developing dream awareness. These pages offer the details for preparation during the first stages of the journey, including pitfalls and surprises you may encounter.

Do you still want to know? Then, let's begin, step by tiny step.

Spiritual Preparation

The stripping away of fears, prejudices, flaws, and all else that interferes with your remembering your primal state is a complex and painful process, but a dreamer gradually understands and *becomes* the meaning. When you have found peace and harmony, the journey will truly make sense.

First, let your life unravel. Snip here and there to let out those tight spaces of the mind that keep the body rigid and seemingly under control. If you already have a dream journal, you know from whence I speak. If you are a beginner, the idea of letting go of control may seem terrifying. Regardless of whether you are a new or experienced dreamer, give yourself a year or longer to fall in love with your inner self, and gradually allow the next level of your journey to be revealed to you. Love surfaces when it is least expected; the point is to trust yourself enough to fall back on your wits as though into the arms of your beloved. Allow your mind to drift and float like a feather falling from the sky—a gentle settling, softly, quietly going down, down, down. The unraveling of our life is part of the journey wherein we begin to recognize that what we have firmly believed was real, is not real at all; certain truths that we have held to be solid and unchanging are actually fragmented and in motion; and what we have relied upon to hold us up in times of trouble, has disappeared. Our values don't hold up, the image of our-self is not real, and there is only one direction to go—forward, until we have reached the other side of duality and been transformed.

Mind-body-spirit connection has subtle movement. Start with simple changes, such as a new hairstyle; or, do something you have always wanted to do, but were reluctant to risk, such as wearing a color not currently in your wardrobe. Something as ordinary as taking a new route to work can open your heart and help you breathe deeply and yield to this invitation.

Friends can join you in this new venture. Ask them over and take your time in fixing a sumptuous, delicious meal, including a rare champagne or sparkling mineral water; use candles, soft lighting, and set an elegant table. Throw caution to the wind and dare yourself to have a feeling heretofore unknown in your range of emotions.

When you are ready—this week, next year, or whenever—ask them what they like about you, and bathe in the warmth of their appreciation. Let them know what you most value about them, too. No risk is too small or insignificant.

You pick and choose the challenge. Your risk can be totally different from these suggestions. Just remember that as you brave venturing into unknown territory in the waking state, you are tilling the soil to bring up the cool, moist earth of your dreams. When your heart and mind have become flexible and pliant, the opening comes.

As a dreamer, or *curandera*—a medicine woman—traveling through your dreamscape, you will find that there is no logical sequence or pattern to your learning. What some dreamers attain in weeks, others may take years to conquer. Movement forward alternates with successes and failures. What is consistent is that to grow spiritually, the dreamer must pay tribute in one form or another.

What you learn, and how you learn, must somehow be reconciled with your outer knowing. A tugging and pulling goes back and forth until one reaches a delicate balance. Your instincts will guide you. How you approach your waking experiences determines what happens in your dreams. And when you have an enlightening dream, remember that growth takes time; the outer and inner must meet on equal footing—no shortcuts, no exceptions.

My Own Beginning

Let me tell you how it happened for me. In 1975, about a year before beginning my dream journals, I began to practice yoga. My body carried tension across my shoulders. Fear and discomfort surrounded me. Years would pass before I was able relax and be comfortable in my body.

In 1982, six years after beginning the journals, I entered a graduate program in counseling at San Francisco State University. I chose to do my internship at the Center for Attitudinal Healing, founded by Jerry Jampolsky, MD, then in Tiburon, California, where I became acquainted with the principles of attitudinal healing. I saw the internship as an opportunity to learn about love.

I also took classes in biofeedback and underwent a radical process called *autogenic training*. Autogenic training is a method of learning to relax the body muscle group by muscle group.

The training in biofeedback also sent me in other directions. In 1983, I was introduced to the Nyingma Institute in Berkeley, California, founded by Rinpoche Tarthang Tulku, where I learned about the flow of energy and how relaxation can aid in the restoration of balance between mind, body, and spirit. Through kum nye relaxation classes, I was able to identify patterns of holding in my body, and this led to my achieving relief from the stress I had been carrying since childhood.

Dreams collaborated by showing me other ways of letting my life unravel. Dream yoga gave me a new perspective on dreaming. Even Grandmother participated by imparting lessons on the necessity of having a resilient mind and body.

If you are a beginner, take your time to explore and find a new relationship with yourself. You will see how important this part of your practice is for remembering where you have been during the night, and you will learn what your next steps in life are to be. What you will witness in your dreams, only time will tell.

If you are an experienced dreamer and already have a spiritual discipline, besides keeping a dream journal, continue doing what you have been doing. A conscious relationship between mind and body is expedient in building the bridge between the waking and sleeping states. Keeping a dream journal is itself a spiritual discipline.

The Journal

Select your journal, and keep it simple. You will need a method and tools you can rely on for the years to come, so keep these practical and accessible. A regular binder with writing paper or a spiral notebook will suffice. Some of my artist friends use large leather-bound sketchbooks for drawing dream scenes that have significance for them. Personally, I have found that entering dream accounts into the computer does not give me the same kinesthetic satisfaction that I get from my hand gliding across the page when writing down the images and fragments that come to mind in the morning. A pen that feels good in your hand is important. Pencil writing becomes hard to read as time passes—it fades and smudges.

Notes on Remembering

Set aside a time to write in the morning; twenty to thirty minutes will probably be enough, maybe less. Relax. Once you have imposed your determination to remember your dreams, details will become more vivid over time.

Whatever the images or feelings that come up, don't dismiss them as trivial or meaningless. In the early stages of dreaming (about the first five years), I saw hundreds of images and had just as many feelings. I became an observer of my internal life. Whatever questions arise for you, just write down what you see, and think about them. Eventually, you will begin to make connections between these seemingly disjointed images. Commit to writing in the morning, and be willing to write merely fragmented memories that come to mind. Just write what you remember. As this awakening happens, my advice is to let it happen without pushing or grasping for it.

As an example of how cryptic notes can be, recording a dream I had in 1976, I wrote only "Lilly and Ernie give G., E., and me some earrings, blue stones."

When I reviewed the journals years later, I realized that I still remembered much more detail. Here is how I remembered the dream many years later.

Remember

My cousins Ernie and Lilly give Georgie, Eleanor, and me some earrings. I hold a tiny gold box in my hand and open it. Two round blue stones. They vibrate and call my attention to something. Like a child's game, they invite me to guess at what they are saying. I feel the stirring of a memory, a vague sense of something wanting to reach out to me.

Again, the stones shake as though saying, "Remember. Remember."
I stare back thinking, "I can't. I can't."

Aside from the sketchy notes, the sensations that came with the shaking of the stones seemed to be jarring something new, an awakening—about culture, and on another level, about the beauty of the true self and of all creation. At the time of the dream, I had no idea what it was attempting to impress upon me. Now, I see it as a spiritual awakening unfolding. I was beginning to remember the deeper essence of *being.*

The Line between Sleeping and Waking

The line between sleeping and waking becomes more complex as the dreamer begins to experience the multidimensional aspects of dreamtime. You are no longer just "asleep" or "awake." Both states of reality take on more expanded meanings. For me, the sensations from the blue stones caused a blurring between the lines of sleeping and waking. I knew "something was happening," and in hindsight, I can see that dreaming awareness was expanding my sense of reality, as though I was caught in an invisible net that simultaneously let me be in both realities at night and during the day.

Spirit Beings Appear

Dream spirits prepare the way for the gift of power, and when they appear to you, they will serve as important guides along the way, but they may also be hiding behind significantly frightening images and feelings. Early stages of record keeping may be filled with a nightmarish quality. Also, nightmares may simply represent our desire to hang on and keep us safe in the familiar. I found that as my body learned to relax, I could go more deeply into the dream and maintain awareness of my breath as my eyes observed events unfolding. This skill did not develop overnight; it took me years, but even so, I saw progress.

Spirit beings that lend a hand can also have a sense of humor. Grandmother's radiant smile, for instance, would nearly shake me awake with its vibrancy, and it always left me in the morning with definite reverberations that reminded me of a Mona Lisa-like smile. Her dancing eyes would literally tease me into playful engagement with her. And there were other beings that caught my attention with their outrageous humor.

The quest evokes many emotional, psychological, and spiritual challenges. When you encounter a dream spirit, take an active stance to find out its purpose in the dream. The spirit being may be there to impart its wisdom.

Disquieting Dreams

In the early stages of dream awareness, you may be apt to forget about the various levels of reality and feel as though the floor is being pulled out from under you. The appearance of a spirit, or finding yourself high off the ground, for example, can be unnerving and cause extreme anxiety. Just remain calm, breathe easily, and maintain awareness of the double state you are in. Breathe deeply.

Experiences will vary. Each dreamer is unique. The decision to become awake within the dream demands fierce determination and the patience of a saint.

Sensory Awareness

Sensory awareness is vital in following this dream map, whether you have your eyes open or have them closed during dreamtime. Your process of becoming aware in your dreams will speed up if in your waking state you practice noticing how your mind drifts to past and future events. Notice whether you can keep your attention on feeling states. Smiles, colors, and a sense of awe or fear are just a few examples of the sensations you will encounter.

In these sensations and impressions, your experience of expanded conscious-ness will leave you breathless. They cannot be described without alluding to the Divine. These sensations are like passports into heaven—there is no other way to describe them. This is what all world religions are about—meeting the Divine. The sensations I've been describing are unmistakable sensations of beauty and joy in all directions. Court them. Treat them gently. Above all, honor them.

If you experience fear, just observe it. Fear, of itself, is neither good nor bad; it is simply a sensation that occurs when something unusual is happening. But fear will become your ally. In my experience, fear became magnified in my dreams as I ventured into new realms. Along with exquisite joy, I commonly experienced naked fear of such intensity that I wanted to abandon a dream or vision. Never-theless, I found it vital to stay within the dream. The intensity of these frightful sensations was a clue that something big was on the other side—something that could only be described as awe.

People in general often believe that by waking up, they bring themselves to safety. But, by staying in the dream, you will always, always, always be rewarded with the bestowal of a sacred gift. To stay within the dream, breathe, focus, and commit to remaining conscious. Expect a reward for your trouble.

I courted these sensations by duplicating them in my waking state: I would wear the colors I saw, or put on an article of clothing similar to something some-one wore in the dream. I also made notes to myself of phrases or images and put them in my working space to remind me of them throughout the day. In some manner or form, I externalized whatever I saw or felt so that I could keep it alive during my waking hours.

I began to appreciate color and combinations of colors more than before beginning the journals. In dreams, red and black became particularly significant, although I did not know what the color combination meant.

If you have a strong affinity to the audio or visual mode of receiving impres-sions, it might help to notice these modes in your dream as well. Paying attention to sensations is important because doing so draws back the curtain between the waking and sleeping states. Equally important, sensory awareness presents a means for restoring communion between mind, body, and spirit.

Here is an example of the subtlety with which these sensations began for me. In 1980, I had the following dream.

Paradise: El Mundo del Rojo y Negro
(The Land of Red and Black)

Leaning on the counter of a concession stand in a huge open marketplace, I consider buying a pair of blue and pink earrings. I decide against them and instead select a pair of beaded blood red and black earrings.

Although not mentioned in the dream, a wonderful sensation of joy resonated for me in a particular way. The dream was straightforward: I was selecting the color combination of dark red and black over the softer blue and pink. Through the sensory experiences, I began to recognize something beautiful and clear through exquisite feelings of knowing.

Community

Doing the work in community is invaluable. We dreamers need to rub our rough edges against others' rough edges and get instant feedback. Participating in a spiritual community will add strength and momentum to your spiritual development.

Over the years, I risked getting close to people in different communities. And although I had thought myself gregarious previously, participating in these communities didn't come naturally. Looking back, I see that the lessons I needed to learn drew me toward and carved a path through a series of involvements in groups. And, like my breath, which feeds me through a rhythm of inhalation and exhalation, over time, the process of sensing inwardly, inquiring, and sharing, advanced the integration of mind, body, and spirit.

Psychotherapist or Spiritual Director

Spiritual transformation requires objectivity. Having an impartial observer to witness your development can be quite helpful. Be willing to stay open to your process without judging it. Life is suffering, and time offers the opportunity to transcend the beliefs of this world. A psychotherapist or spiritual director can assist you in advancing your spiritual development.

Spiritual Self

A dream I had while studying at the Nyingma Institute encouraged me not to confuse my feelings with my spiritual self. My teacher, who appears in the dream, was the dean of the institute at the time. He is a dreamer, and I had recently taken a dream workshop from him.

Es Necesario
(It's Necessary)

A friend and I drive in my blue '72 Dodge Dart with A., who is sitting in the back seat. In the front passenger's seat, I turn around and face him.

As though he is telling the funniest joke, he blurts out with an infectious laughter, "Your feelings are essential to your spiritual growth. There's no way around them." With a twinkle in his eye, he adds, "And, watch out for those surprises."

When I relayed the dream to the dean in class, he looked at me quizzically for a moment, and then he said, "Those are Rinpoche's exact words to me." Rinpoche Tarthang Tulku[14] was known for having a sense of humor on serious matters. This was especially appropriate to my need. My feelings were markedly apparent during the time I practiced there, yet I still tried to pretend I was above them. I often felt a sense of shame or embarrassment when my feelings spilled out. As much as I loathe admitting this today, it took many a year to learn this lesson.

The Paradigm Shift

For a dreamer of the Western world, this dream map presents a different paradigm, a multidimensional perception of the world, a view that is vastly different from Western psychology. In its broadest sense, Western psychology holds that dreams are a reflection of the dreamer's unconscious or deeper issues. Carl Jung, a student of Freud (and a serious dreamer), believed dreams offered a glimpse into a personal behavior, the unconscious pondering of a life issue, or an isolated dilemma present in one's life. However, he also developed the theory of the collective unconscious that holds that the individual is born with all the thoughts and feelings of not only one's ancestors, but of the entire human race. Jung's theories can be complementary to your process and taken into consideration in understanding your dreams, particularly if you choose to work with the Jungian theory of the Shadow.[15] Jung thought of the Shadow as a part of our personal makeup that is disowned and surfaces in ways we do not recognize as part of ourselves. An example would be an artist who ignores her talent or creative urges, becomes an art dealer, and then wonders how she became involved in selling other artists' work. These lost parts of you play a vital role throughout the stages of transformation.

From the spiritual perspective of this dream map, however, dreaming is quite different from the Western model, because of the difference in worldviews or paradigms. This dream map sees "awakening" as remembering who we truly are in spirit when we see ourselves reflected in the creation of the universe. We are not the body—frail, vulnerable, and suffering. We are not our feelings—which reflect our responses to what our caretakers projected upon us. Reality lies in the spirit world, which is multidimensional. We are spirit, and we have a great deal of freedom when we can view dreamtime as reality, and life on Earth as the dream.

Inner Teacher

Experiences that are actual journeys into other dimensions present themselves in dreams, and the spirits you encounter are as real as the people you meet in the waking state. A spirit being may leave a message and be gone just as quickly as he or she appeared. Or, a relationship with an inner teacher such as the one I developed with Grandmother may take on a life of its own.[16] One or both can emerge.

Discipline

Many paths lead to transformation, and dreaming is only one of them. In my inquiries into world religions, I have found that the flow of energy is a vital aspect in understanding the will of the Divine for our lives. Dreaming, as understood in the Mesoamerican traditions, is a path of awakening through extended alertness and wakefulness in our dreamtime. In much the same way, yoginis and yogis of India utilize the power of kundalini, Asian traditions focus on the activity of chi, and the Desert Fathers of the Christian tradition approached communion through surrender. What I'm saying here is that the mind needs to be flexible and supple, open to different possibilities. Through discipline and intention, dreamers achieve surrender through resilient minds and bodies.

Physical disciplines, including yoga, kum nye, and chi kung, and others can help you transcend your ego. These practices teach us to become aware that in our bodies, we are holding patterns that also exist in our personalities. These patterns are subtle, and it may take some time before you achieve mind/body integration. Relaxed minds and bodies are essential as we approach dreaming.

Another discipline is working with one's mind and learning to disengage from thoughts that modify our concepts of possibilities. In the 1980s, my brother John gave me a copy of *A Course in Miracles,*[17] a workbook with a particular Christian perspective teaching that only love is real. Since then, I have studied the 365 daily lessons several times, and these lessons have influenced the way I look at the world. Similar to the way the Old Dreamers saw life as the dream, the *Course* also sees the waking world as illusion.

Various spiritual study groups abound that you can join to facilitate a new frame of reference by which to see reality.

Summary

This chapter has discussed the process of opening up to your inner self and commencing the process of uniting mind, body, and spirit. Beginning the journal and finding a comfortable way of ending your night with twenty to thirty minutes of writing is easy; it's the stripping away of the familiar that presents the challenge.

Be practical in your selection of writing materials. Take your time, and be consistent in your writing practice. Your awareness of reality will shift. Surround yourself with support, community, psychotherapy, and/or spiritual direction. What you are entering into is an ancient tradition—as ancient as the world—and it has a timing of its own.

Stay with your feelings within the dream. Fear and awe wait. Distinguish between your waking self and the Self that begins to emerge. Recognize that you are making a transition from psychological/waking time focus to a spiritual focus where the inner is more real than the waking. Keep in mind that a spiritual discipline such as yoga or slow movement will facilitate mind, body, and spirit integration. Enter your dreams as consciously as possible, noticing the levels of relaxation, with mind, body, and spirit becoming one. In waking and sleeping, be aware of your senses, noticing smiles, color, feelings of awe and fear. When we slowly enter a cool pool of water, there comes a tipping point when we surrender, even if against our will, and then it's all or nothing.

And, finally, dreaming is like creating a beautiful tapestry of hundreds of satin, silk, linen threads and ribbons of many colors—reds, blues, yellows—textures of feelings, sweet fragrances, and elements woven together. Some strands appear in waking time, but in dreamtime, appear only for a millisecond and then are gone; and other textures, sensations and colors we see abundantly in dreams, but in waking life, they disappear, just as stars fade with the light of coming day. We sometimes miss completely the threads of gold, silver, and copper that we weave into this great tapestry, but they are always there, surfacing and then going back underground with the beating of the heart.

I offer these guidelines as a rough format in directing your course toward your awakening within the dream. Remember that the world you have entered into is more real than the waking world; indeed, at some point, it will become apparent that the inner world is more solid than the waking. Allow it to approach you with its grace and compassion—let go. Trust yourself.

You will be tested. You are going into the unknown and will find many a strange thing. Be attentive.

Abrazos y buena suerte. "Hugs, and good luck." E-mail me now and then.[18]

CHAPTER 2

▼

Naming It: Before Dawn

Without the following event, I am not sure I would have ever plumbed the depths of my dreams. It had to be a deep yearning that pushed me toward communion with something greater than I had found in conventional religion. In spite of the Hunger and loneliness I felt at the time, I thought I was content with the status quo of my life.

I've met very few people in my excursions who inquire into the nature of their nocturnal adventures, into those things that happen during the hours when the body is in a neutral mode, at rest but receptive. Here and there I have found artists, mystics, and *curanderas* who were daring enough to plunge in, and I've seen twinkles, a sense of knowing, in their eyes that betray their secret. But without being pushed into it, I am not certain I would have embarked on this path.

Ostracized

The event that steadily and relentlessly beat a drum beneath the surface of my consciousness had a subtle but long-lasting impact on my perceptions of religion. This was the day I was excluded from reading two Bible verses in Sunday school when I was in my early teens.

Back for the first time after months of living in Berkeley with a pastor and his family while my mother worked, I noticed the new constellation of friendships among my friends as they walked in front of me, and the new dresses I hadn't seen before. I was acutely aware that no one was walking beside me. We had a new young pastor who spoke English—which was a pronounced departure from the universal Spanish we spoke in church—and for some reason, he was our teacher that day. He asked his pupils to read from the Bible, and I was among the last three. There were six verses left. He told Paul on my right to read three, skipped over me, and had Sarah on my left read three. *Silly me*, I was wearing lipstick, a taboo that I, in my growing rebelliousness, had violated. Then, the following evening, I was ostracized from the choir.

I told my parents about the incidents, and their solution was for me to invite myself to go with my friend Mary to her white, middle-class Episcopal Church downtown. It turned out that Mary preferred not to go, and we found a diner to escape to. I welcomed the chance to avoid the disconnectedness I always felt when in a crowd of people.

My Mother's Death

But then worse things came. A year later, my mother died, and that severed whatever fragile ties remained to my old spiritual community. My mother's death also demolished what little foundation had been left for me to stand on. It robbed me of the feminine in my life, and soon I was being forced to think in logical, linear male terms.

Within six months, I moved to a women's residence. I rarely spoke Spanish in the big city, San Francisco, which became my new home. At that time, I didn't realize that my interest in the metaphysical had been connected to my culture, but with the passing years, the dissonance became more apparent, and a desperate need to bond to a group that truly resonated for me began to grow. I hadn't bargained for reestablishing ties with my past. And then *she* came. After changes of such magnitude, Grandmother's arrival was the grounding force I needed to regain my strength. I wanted and needed an ally.

Corn Woman's Legacy

One of the creation stories[19] illustrates Corn Woman's legacy to us—the message of rebirth and transformation. Corn Woman's message resounds with a complex constellation of goddesses and transcending dimensions that provide us with opportunities for awakening.

The story begins with Corn Woman's role in the life of her grandsons, a pair of twins she is rearing. Tired of their diet of deer meat, the boys wonder aloud if Grandmother could oblige them with a new dish for the evening's meal. The boys go off on their hunting for the day, and Corn Woman sets about on her task of creating the requested new dish. Through her power of creation, she manifests a vegetable by shaking herself and peeling kernels of corn off her skin. That evening, the new vegetable is an astounding success, adding new dimensions to the steady diet of deer meat. The story meanders through the minds of the young men and one of them determines that the next day he will unearth the secrets of this mysterious new dish.

All goes according to plan, and a few days later the boys discover Grandmother's magic. When she *sees* that the boys have been spying on her, she decides that it is time for her to leave them so that they may use the new food to build their own lives. She announces that she will be leaving them, and outlines the details of what they are to do with her body.

The time comes for Corn Woman to leave this world, and she reminds her grandsons that they will kill her by cutting her head off, and posting it above the entrance to her house. Then they are to drag her body over the fields, bury it, and thereupon a cornstalk shall appear the following spring.

In directing that her head be cut off, Corn Woman teaches us to transcend duality; by having her head posted at the highest point of the house, she lets us know that she will watch over all of humanity; and in her self-sacrifice, she leaves a staple by which to nourish her children and be remembered throughout eternity.

Herein lies the key to transformation that I found within the religions of the Americas. Corn Woman's sacrifice, the cutting off of her head reveals that, not the body, but *consciousness* is the doorway toward transformation. The staple she leaves behind is sacred, must be treated as such, and remembered for its message.

Duality and Transformation

Transformation requires a bridging of many facets of the old cultures, and duality is one of them. Of the early gods, the God of Duality provided the most opportunities for spiritual evolvement. The Aztecs paired the Mexican gods representing the four cardinal points with aspects of nature, and they believed that in the oppositions, such as strengths and weaknesses, lay the secrets of renewal.

Quetzalcoatl, the lord of compassion and his nemesis, *Texcatlipoca*, lord of night, represented the east and west, respectively. These examples of opposing forces, together with each individual force, illustrate the significance of duality and the challenges they pose in aspiring to rebirth.[20]

Duality was also found in the Mayan quadrants of the Four Directions that incorporated the concepts of time and space and rejuvenation. The Four Directions and the levels above and below were alive with the sacred.[21]

The God of Duality

The Mesoamerican sacred texts of the Mayan and Aztec Creation Stories within the *Popol Vuh*[22] tell us that before there was time and word, there was only stillness, silence, water, and pitch-blackness. The early gods we meet in the history of Mesoamerica cover a wide range of functions and symbolic meaning. The dream existed, and nothing existed outside of it. The God of Duality sat supreme at the apex of the early cosmology: Maker, Modeler, Bearer, Begetter, Xpiyacoc (the masculine face of God) and Xmucané, Corn Woman (the feminine face of God). They set their thoughts to dreaming of humans who would be capable of remembering and worshiping them.

In Mesoamerica, the names are difficult to keep track of because the Maya and Aztecs had the same cosmology but had distinct names for their gods. Corn Woman went by many other names. *Ometecuhtli* was an early name for her, but in her most striking pose, Corn Woman emerges as *Coatlicue*, "Filth Eater," and Serpent Skirt, and as such, she appears as a wild, cosmic eater of human hearts. These seemingly negative names have been greatly misunderstood. In its broadest terms, her essence incorporates life *and* death. But she also absorbs our human foibles and has compassion for human suffering. It was said that without her, there would be no bridge to heaven, and mankind could not exist.[23]

By the time the Spaniards arrived in Mesoamerica, the goddess *Tonantzín*, had succeeded Coatlicue, and was known as the goddess of compassionate protection of the people; and when the Catholic Church accepted her in the early 1500s, she was incorporated as *La Virgen de Guadalupe*, our Mother of Compassion. Across North America in particular, creation stories abound that seem to have a common thread weaving the goddesses together with the stories of Mesoamerica. Corn Woman appears by different names, including Spider Woman, Changing Woman, Thought Woman, and many others.[24]

The contrasts in the God of Duality, as reflected in legends, were symbolic of many aspects of the Mesoamerican cosmology. In the opposites lay the avenue to conversion. In the battles between good and evil, the opposites laid the foundation for striving toward an understanding beyond the struggle, as though they were pointing toward the solution. Duality stood for the negative and positive and the male and female principles in the universe, as well as light and shadow, yes and no, night and day, above and below, east and west, and life and death.[25] Fathoming the depths of the God of Duality in one's life was of prime importance.

For today's dreamer to comprehend duality, her experience must undergo some interpretation, and this is where a paradigm shift is necessary. In our dreams we see and experience other dimensions, and the dream figures we encounter are as real and valid as those in our waking state.

As you, the dreamer, reach deeper states of awareness, you will feel emotional pain more acutely, and moments of sheer ecstasy will also be magnified. These extremes constitute duality. Maturity teaches us that all aspects of our lives and the perceptions we hold to be true often are reflections of the small self or ego. And, thankfully, ideas that ordinary awareness holds as true are dismantled as we "move through" duality.

In the old cultures, pain and suffering were seen as stemming from dualistic beliefs. Power emerges for the *curandera*/artist from identification with the Creatrix, and helps her to transcend these painful aspects of duality. Transcendence facilitates the creation of art, dance, music, poetry, drumming, healing, or other gifts. When you have shed the "self" by overcoming duality, awakening is possible, and helpful spirits abound to help you along in this journey.

In my life, suffering through the tensions of duality brought me to the rock-bottom places where I connected with the disturbing self-images that I was so reluctant to face. But, in my dreams there was concrete assistance and validation for overcoming them.

In an ideal world, an older, more experienced dreamer guides the beginner through the painful unearthing of hidden aspects of character—aspects the dreamer needs to see in the light of day and give to Spirit for healing and rejuvenation. Agony and profound healing go hand in hand. Having an objective witness celebrating this stage of our spiritual growth can propel us on to successful completion of the task, and in that completion, we will find true liberation. Also, having someone to remind us of the spiritual abundance and the help available facilitates the task.

Corn Woman's role cannot be separated from confrontation with duality—spiritual awakening; the concept of duality and her message are inextricably woven together. As, we will see in the coming chapters, the resultant gift from our confrontation with duality is power, which coincides with what her role in the Creation Stories models for us.

The Way to Transformation

The complexity of the Mesoamerican cosmology and the functions of the gods reflect the intricacies of transformation. In my study, I found at least three religious practices, other than transcending duality, through which transformation could be achieved: undergoing trial by fire; entering the multidimensionality of time and space; and the arduous practice of nagualismo.

Through Fire

Fire was an avenue for seeking transformation. The story of Quetzalcoatl tells us that Quetzalcoatl, also known as the Feathered Serpent, suffered bitterly in life. When he found himself persecuted and abandoned, he chose to jump into the fire as a way to leave behind a lesson about the dream of life.

While on his way toward his final transformation, he traveled the underworld to create the means through which we humans could continue our path of awakening. When his tasks were completed, he was transformed into the Morning Star, Venus, the First Light of Day, and the First Light of Night.[26]

Quetzalcoatl's spirit was especially alive and vibrant in the Light. This was the level of spirituality the ancestors aspired toward in building their pyramids so precisely, so that every spring, the light of Venus, symbolizing his spirit, would be framed in their midst.

Through Transcending Time and Space

Another avenue through which the Mesoamericans sought transformation was by transcending time and space. Awakening in the spirit induces seeing with our spiritual eyes, and our relationship with the Divine is affirmed. All this happens in other levels of reality: the spaces above the world, and the spaces below—in the spirit world, and when the spirit world itself opens to us.

The Mayan concept of time, a very difficult one to explain, is known as "the action of *kinh.* "[27] For the Maya and Aztecs, time was imbued with the spirit of a deity that made time sacred and ever present, ever now.[28]

The story of *La Virgen de Guadalupe*[29] is an example of time and space in action. As the story has been told, in 1512, a humble peasant named Juan Diego was on his way to market when he came upon a beautiful woman who spoke to him and asked him to speak to the local bishop and request the construction of her temple on the site where she stood. At first, the magnificent presence terrified Juan Diego, for he realized the woman was of another world. As she continued to speak to him, he regained his composure and was able to affirm the reality of his senses. In time he succeeded in carrying out her request, because she gave him tangible evidence to take to the bishop—a huge bouquet of red roses. The *Basílica* of *La Virgen de Guadalupe* now stands where she appeared to Juan Diego.[30] The spirit being's appearing to Juan Diego in the waking world is an example of transcendence of time and space.

Through Nagualismo/Transmutation

Transmutation—which means changing a substance into something else—also known as shape-shifting or metamorphosis, changing oneself into another form, was a part of the beliefs of the Mesoamericans. In many instances, the actions of the gods in the heavens impacted the nature of reality in this dimension in hugely dramatic ways. They actually traveled through time and space and shape-shifted, leaving these as examples for us to follow.

The stories of transmutation left many clues to remind future generations of the greatness and power of the universe. The stories include many magnificent deeds performed by the gods, such as when *Ometecuhtli*, "gave birth to a knife of hard stone that she threw to Earth, and 1,600 heroes were born."[31] In this instance, she created the stars. This act of the Goddess was code for the magnitude of power available to dreamers who could succeed in duplicating the actions of the gods. I cannot overstate the importance of the role of the Goddess; she offers a vital image of the feminine in both power and creation—especially in power. The Catholic Church, however, has supplanted this image, though still powerful, with the milder figure of Mary who is *mother only.*

Quetzalcoatl was a great shape-shifter in the legends of Mesoamerica. Throughout history in the Americas, Quetzalcoatl was known as a god/king, an artist, and had many other identities as well. But the members of the nobility were often named Quetzalcoatl, so there tends to be confusion between legend and history. He went by many names throughout the Americas, including *Guku-matz, Kukulkan, Itzamna*, and many others.[32]

We see other examples of shape-shifting in *The Story of Quetzalcoatl.*[33] In one version of this story, I found at least seven examples. Three wizards, *Huitzilo-*

pochtli, Titlacauan, and *Tlacauepan,* are mentioned, and through their appearances and activities, they demonstrate their ability to shape-shift.

The first wizard, Titlacauan, performs various acts of wizardry—such as turning himself into an old man and then into a young Huaxtec to charm Quetzalcoatl's daughter. Next, with the beat of his drum, he created a trancelike atmosphere of merriment and led the children of the village to the edge of the cliffs where they fell to their death. In another instance, he changed himself into an unrecognizable individual who lured the people into a similar trance; by so doing, he caused great destruction to the Toltec (950–1150 CE) and many died.

From stories like these came the religious beliefs and spiritual aspirations of the early cultures. The *Tlamitimines,* the Old Dreamers, duplicated these great feats, and were led closer to freedom.[34]

Summary

As conveyed through Corn Woman's legacy, the message is that we are to strive toward transformation. In our struggles with duality, we can transcend the limitations of this dimension. In a world of contrasts, the Mesoamerican gods reflected themselves in legends of transformation in which they transcend duality through time and space, and nagualismo. Ometecuhtli created the stars by throwing a knife into space; Quetzalcoatl transcended duality through fire, but he left for us a symbolic model by which to transcend—travel through the deeper levels of consciousness. In the battles between the forces from above and below, the legends laid the foundation for striving toward an understanding beyond the struggle, as though the legends were pointing out the solution.

Fathoming the depths of the God of Duality was of prime significance in life. Today, we can transcend duality through awareness of the reality of other dimensions, time and space; and in the development of spiritual power through the practices of nagualismo. The resultant power for us as dreameers of today can then be applied to our lives as *curanderas*/healers, writers, musicians, scientists, and so on. The gift is power that manifests in enduring relationships within and beyond our art for the benefit of our communities. As it relates to the legacy of Corn Woman, the staple of corn becomes a sacred symbol and reminder that we can, through our art, strive toward and attain higher levels of spirituality for the benefit of all humanity. When we succeed, we receive her blessing, and Corn Woman is highly pleased.

Corn Woman's message is a bright light that shines forth from the past as a call to transformation. Recognition of the validity of her message for our lives actually rekindles our connection to the past, and understanding the past's cultural paradigm is paramount. This is what I found, and this is the message I hope to pass on to you. Many gifts abound here, especially identification with the power of the feminine.

Seeing the complexity of their religion, one can understand the need for a priesthood and sages who could translate the spiritual teachings for the layperson.

That the stars were created by a goddess struck a chord within me. It stood in bold contrast to the idea of their having been created by the masculine god I had been taught to believe in. When I discovered that *my* identity could be blended with such power, I was reborn. *What a shocking difference lies between the two beliefs.* In this respect, Corn Woman gives power as well as the means to move beyond our earthly identity and struggles. If we are daughters of greatness of that magnitude, then that likeness reverberates through our own acts of creation.

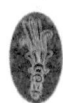

▼

CHAPTER 3

The World of the Dreamer

"I am as real here as you are standing there."

Having once recognized Corn Woman's message as a call for transformation and its concomitant power, I began to redefine my relationship with God. I felt much more responsible for uncluttering my mind and purifying my motives in order to be of service in my community. I myself became responsible for dissolving the obstacles that separated me from all creation—feelings of sadness, disappointment, rage, and selfishness—became my responsibility to resolve. In the old traditions, I had found models and building blocks to fill my own spiritual needs.

The *curandera* (dreamer) needs a dream map to define her journey in this world—where the line between dimensions is thin and permeable, and in which all matter is vibrant with the power of creation. Knowledge of dream traditions of the past can serve to point the way along the various avenues of transformation and define appropriate markers for navigating on our voyages. We can learn from the examples our cultural ancestors left for us.

The Tlamitamines

The traditional figures who could speak with authority came from the Maya and Aztec (*Nahua*) religions. Nahua, a word which means "one who speaks with authority," was "the name of the linguistic group of people inhabiting the central Mexican plateau.'"[35] Persons believed to be diviners were those "whose authority is believed to come from the gods who give them insight into creation, and power to make cosmic forces work for and not against the well-being of mankind."[36] At the time of the Spanish conquest, the persons who held this tradition were known as the *Tlamitamines, the Old Dreamers.*

In the Aztec culture, Tlamitamines trained formally in schools on such spiritual matters as dreaming and traveling outside the body. Where the supernatural and the mundane merged, the dreamers/priests had their role defined for them. Traveling between the spaces and knowledge of each realm was a matter of seeing at the deeper levels of reality.[37] In these disciplines, they sought freedom from duality and aspired toward transformation. The initiates who learned to travel between the worlds were awarded the distinguished privilege of wearing the color combination of red and black, a right reserved for the spiritually gifted.[38] People of the red and black cloth were then seen as the spiritual elite.

Before the European cultures arrived, the role and influence of dreamers in the Mesoamerican cultures varied widely and ran deep. The dreamers served as statesmen and government counselors, educators, healers, priests, artists, and warriors. They served as psychologists and counseled individuals, leading them through the process of transcending duality; this passage was known as "giving a face and heart." "Face and heart" also included the development of character and the divining of the individual's destiny.

The Tlamitamines were celibate and lived their lives within their educational setting and away from their families. Tlamitamines were selected for their role because of their strength of character and purity of heart, and they came from all walks of life.[39]

The horrifying murder of thousands of dreamers who had predicted the demise of the Aztec Empire illustrates that they were commonly included in political affairs, and that event appears to mark the end of their predominance. For the previous ten years, dreamers and *Moctezuma*, the then-ruling king of the Aztecs, had been reporting dreams that predicted the arrival of strangers who would bring drastic consequences to their world as they knew it. As *Moctezuma* sought to allay his deepest fears, he called his dreamers and magicians together. When none offered a glimmer of hope, he ordered them slain. Researchers believe that ten thousand dreamers were killed.[40]

This story becomes more poignant when viewed as the beginning of the deadly silence that fell upon the peoples of the Americas in the aftermath of the massive and profound destruction of the native cultures when they collided with the European cultures. Had *Moctezuma* heeded the words of his dreamers and other advisors, he could have prepared for what would come. In their world, dreamers were the chroniclers of the past and the future; their counsel was vital to ensure their world's continued existence.[41]

Books of the Red and Black Ink, left by generations of Tlamitamines and other sages, define in minute detail their role in the Mesoamerican cultures. These books contained information that enabled Tlamitamines to prescribe hallucinogenic plants in their healing and dreaming practices, described incantations for healing, and, very importantly, bestowed upon the dreamer the power to intercede between the common person and the Divine. These books included information on how to predict the future, reveal the past, and how to shape-shift. They discussed how to live in a world where interactions between the dimensions were common. From consultation and ritual with a Tlamitamin, an empowered seeker had the tools to live out his or her destiny as determined by the God of Duality.[42]

Throughout this dream map, we will be exploring the native worldview. In this chapter, we will be exploring this worldview to understand the practices and exercises in the coming chapters.

Duality

The Aztecs and the Mayans gave the term "duality" to the process of going through darkness. As initiates worked out the conflicts inherent in duality, they came to another stage, which was called getting a "face and heart." Transcendence and transformation were the reward of the seeker, the dreamer who was prepared to go to any extreme to unite with truth. Transcendence was attained through arduous labor, strenuous discipline, and dedication.

The counsel that Tlamitamines gave initiates—guidance and encouragement—opened opportunities for transcending duality. In the journeys that they traveled, sometimes with the aid of herbs, the initiates underwent challenges that helped them to recognize the dissonance within their characters. From these teachings, the initiates developed character that deepened awareness of their destiny and strengthened their understanding and communion with the Divine.

The Old Dreamers' process allowed them to detach from the "laws" of society and the waking life so they could stand face-to-face with eternity, timelessness, and the Divine. As mentioned in the first chapter, the dream will struggle to be forgotten; thus to blend their dreams with their waking life, the Old Dreamers had to have a fierce determination to remember minute details of their dreams. The tasks they performed in traveling through duality demanded their utmost and undivided attention.

Time and Space

As Irwin, a researcher in North American Plains Indians' dreaming, points out, the space in which dreamers live needs explanation, because of the multidimensional aspects of the dream world.[43]

The Nahua saw the world as divided into quadrants. These quadrants referred to the visionary topography of the spiritual world. The east was symbolized by the color red; the south, by the color yellow; the west, black; and the north, white. Crocodile, also known as Earth Monster, and The Bacabs held up the four quadrants of the sky. Within this topography, a horizontal hierarchy existed. These horizontal spaces were defined as the thirteen realms of heaven upward, and the nine realms of the land of the dead that lay below.

By the same principle, nature reflected the aliveness of the power of creation. Through "knowing," nature became enlivened and communicated with humanity—stones could speak, for example. The aliveness of mountains, rivers, trees, and all animal life held the sacred consciousness of the Great Mystery and would also communicate with human beings.

When the priests (the Old Dreamers) invoked the presence of the spirits, they expected visible and tangible results. They did not plead with their gods—rather, they commanded them. The Old Dreamers had the power to make manifest on Earth what came from above. With ceremony, methodical repetition which enabled them to reach altered states of consciousness, use of incense and incantation, they called the powers from above into this world:

> Crocodile of the red quadrant,
> Come to me,
> Thirteen are the waters
> Of my red gutter,

When I guard my rear
Behind the east sky

Crocodile of the white quadrant,
Come to me,
Thirteen are the waters
Of my white gutter
When I guard my rear
Behind the north sky

Crocodile of the black quadrant,
Come to me,
Thirteen are the waters
Of my black gutter
When I guard my rear
Behind the west sky

Crocodile of the yellow quadrant,
Come to me,
Thirteen are the waters
Of my yellow gutter
When I guard my rear
Behind the south sky[44]

These spirits made their reality known in ceremony and ritual, and as mentioned earlier, through uses of mind-altering herbs. As Irwin[45] explained, their reality was not intended for interpretation into Western terms. For these levels and directions embraced beings and entities more real to the native cultures than the structure of a building or an object held in one's hand. The dreamer and the culture "saw" or "knew" the reality of these beings.

Carlos Castaneda offered an explanation about the multidimensionality of the universe according to Don Juan, his Yaqui teacher: "New worlds exist! [Levels of reality] are wrapped one around the other, like the skins of an onion. The world we exist in is but one of these skins."[46]

An example of multidimensionality and interaction between dreamer and spirit beings can be seen in the dream of a slave woman in central Mexico shortly before the arrival of the Spaniards. In her dream, a goddess came to the slave woman and advised her of the cataclysmic changes that would occur with the arrival of strangers. An eagle carried the woman to a plateau where "the gods of the universe" met her and advised her to convey a message to the local ruler. She was to advise him to destroy the kettledrums, stop sacrifices, and prepare for the devastation of the land.

In addition to multidimensionality, this dream reveals inter-dimensional travel. The sages of the time believed that the dreamer had visited spirit beings in another realm. When she awoke in the morning, she found herself at the edge of a precipice. She began her trek home, which took her a full day and part of the night. She arrived home at midnight.[47]

This dream also serves as an example of seeing the future in dreams. Within the space of three years from this dream, the order of the culture was drastically altered by the arrival of the Spaniards, and there were many other examples of foreseeing the future throughout the culture: .[48]

Through this understanding of the sacredness of time and space, the Old Dreamers not only felt the power of the eternal now, but in this collapse of the ordinary world, they communed with beings that informed and guided their lives toward awakening.[49]

Nagualismo

According to Castaneda,[50] a dreamer acquired the ability to control his/her "assemblage point." Don Juan, Castaneda's teacher, described the human being as a luminous ball with a point of "intense brilliance" the size of a tennis ball within the outer luminous shell. This point resides "about two feet back from the crest of a person's right shoulder blade." The Toltec (950–1150 CE) saw that the assemblage point had a number of filaments passing through it, and that these greatly intensified the point. They also saw that displacement of the assemblage point from its natural position was key to controlling their appearance.

> Don Juan said that the older sorcerers [dreamers] proposed that in human beings, the assemblage point, by focusing its glowing sphere on the universe's filaments of energy that pass directly through it, automatically and without premeditation assembles those filaments into a steady perception of the world.[51]

In other words, through control of the assemblage point, dreamers had the ability to change themselves into whatever form they had practiced being seen as. But, Castaneda points out that the agenda of the dreamers had changed from

attempting to have control over others to opting for their own personal transformation.

Power

When a dreamer receives a transfer of power from a spirit being, animal, or natural substance—such as stone, water, or mountain—she may thereafter develop
the ability to perform some feat not otherwise commonly performed by humans.
This gift may be the ability to see the future, heal the sick, or in some way be of
benefit to the community.[52] As an example, those to whom the ghost was said to
have shown compassion are able to anticipate death.[53] Another example is the
ability to transcend duality through the power of the eagle, wherein one goes
beyond the struggle of human existence and lives in the essence of the moment.[54]

Spanish Conquest

The Spanish conquest of Mexico in the 1500s split the role of the Tlamitamines
into two paths. Under the tyranny of the Catholic Church, one strand went
underground because it was unsafe to continue the old traditions.

The other strand chose a path directly into the priesthood of the new religion
of the Americas. In their capacity as priests of the Catholic Church, the dreamers
asserted their influence by weaving in stories that would keep active the memory
of the multidimensional world.[55]

North American Dreamers

Irwin[56] tells of a cedar tree spirit who appeared in the form of a woman to Roaming Chief, a Pawnee Indian. Initially, Roaming Chief heard the singing, and
upon finding the singer, he spoke to her. Conveying a song to him, she again
merged with the tree, wherein she continued to sing the song. The Bear Society
then used in its ceremonies the songs that Roaming Chief received. As the melody was sung, Mother Cedar's presence came forth to recreate the sacredness of
the vision.

North American dreamers continue to this day to have similar traditions that
honor the multidimensionality of the universe. As shown in their practices of
vision quests, understanding ritual and interaction with spirit beings requires
preparation and training. At times, especially for women, meetings with the
sacred and/or travel into other worlds occur spontaneously.[57]

Their Future Is Now

The Tlamitamines foresaw the shift in consciousness, and they predicted that by the year 2011 CE, there would be a resurgence of consciousness as they had always known it. Through their computations, the Mesoamerican dreamers foretold that a great change would take place 453 years into the future. They talked about earthquakes as code for a time for great change, as in a rebirth or renewed power.[58]

The predicted time frame has arrived. In the past sixty years, there has been a surfacing of information about the old cultures that heretofore had been unavailable.

As evidenced in the work of contemporary Chicana writers, dreamers, and *curanderas*, some still have the wisdom—buried as it is—here in *El Norte*.[59]

For example, in 1989, I was living in Hawaii when I received news that a long-time friend had transitioned into her next life. That night I retired early for bed, but unable to sleep, I got up and went outside. Very clearly, as I stood outside, quietly chanting an ancient Tibetan death song, I experienced an opening between this and another dimension.

The event gave me pause; the line between dimensions is still permeable, and the world in which the Old Dreamers lived is not far away at all.

I made the following entry in my journal.

El Arbolito
(The Tree)

I slowly and softly began a chant I learned at the Nyingma Institute. Suddenly, I heard a noise like a thud on the roof of the house, and I turned around, thinking my then-husband had joined me. No one was at the door, but with light from the moon, I could see a tall figure standing on the roof. The odd part was that I couldn't tell where the figure began and the palm tree that stood outside the door ended.

I stopped chanting. Focusing my eyes as much as I could, I thought to myself, Now, this is interesting—I think there is a giant on the roof, and I'm standing down here thinking he's smiling at me.

"I'm as real here as you are standing there," I heard him say clearly in my head.

Without moving or turning my head, I darted my eyes around to see whether everything else looked normal. A huge eucalyptus at the edge of the yard seemed to be emitting a soft glow, and the leaves looked like satin ribbons tied in bows. The light vibrated within me and caused a sensation of indescribable joy. I maintained my stillness.

Resuming the chanting, I kept my watch. As in a dream, I tried to stretch the moment out as long as possible. After several minutes, the image faded, and my eyes returned to their usual mode of "seeing."

It is important to note that I was in a state of reverie as I chanted. When I gazed up at the figure standing on the roof, his words were crystal clear to me, and I had no doubt as to their validity—*"I am as real here as you are standing there."*

The soft glow in different parts of the yard indicated to me that I had entered an altered state of consciousness. But today, I actually believe that my chanting may have called the spirit being to me, much as the Old Dreamers, while in ceremony, commanded spirits to their service. As I chanted, they heard my song as an invitation to join me in this dimension. Surprisingly, I found the exact words spoken to me by the spirit being quoted in an old text.[60]

Summary

Chapter 2 and this chapter highlight the spiritual beliefs of the cultures prior to the arrival of the Europeans and demonstrate how the Old Dreamers lived out these beliefs. For these cultures, reality lay in the spiritual realms. Their worldview was multidimensional.

As this chapter illustrates, the Old Dreamers saw their world within worlds, possibility beyond possibility. They traveled inter-dimensionally, communed with spirit beings from the Four Directions, and communicated with nature. Playing a wide range of roles within different cultures, the Old Dreamers' power was defined by strength of character and ability to cure, see, dream, shape-shift, and predict the future.

As I pointed out earlier, at the time of the Spanish conquest, the Old Dreamers' tradition was split into two paths: those who went underground and continued to provide guidance and direction for the future of the culture, and priests who went into the Catholic Church and influenced the structuring of the Catholic Church in Mexico.

The stories that we hear about the Old Dreamers' greatness seem somewhat fantastic, but there are leftovers of the practice of nagualismo as seen in tthe writings of Castaneda. Feats of nagualismo have been modified or redirected toward freedom and transformation. Emphasis is no longer placed on magical feats, but, rather, on transcending duality/darkness.

The world of dreams is vast and wide, and any variety of experiences can confront and take us into unknown worlds. Multidimensionality, inter-dimensional travel and seeing the future are available to us today. Eventually, we come to see the dream world as the Tlamitamines saw it—as more solid than the waking world.

The key to bear in mind about the Old Dreamers' view of the universe is that they saw all of life as imbued with the power of creation. They believed that their presence at the time of creation had imbued them with extraordinary powers.

As our practice of dreaming evolves, we begin to understand their paradigm. Just as the Old Dreamers traveled multi-dimensionally, we see that other worlds are opening up to us. Stepping into our world of dreams, we will also find the vastness of their universe. Wise Ones will take an active part in our dream lives to help us awaken and reach the ultimate reality. Their instruction is vibrant, incredibly wise, and tangibly accessible.

In the following chapters, I will illustrate how our destiny manifests through our dreams, and how you can bring forth sacred gifts destined for you only. This message of transformation will ring true for you. There are many ways in which life will force us toward transcending our particular demons of darkness. Small and large decisions and changes in the direction of your life will happen. It's a foregone conclusion that life changes will happen the way they're supposed to. Your path will be illuminated, and the only choice you will face is whether to be transformed or not. When the need to awaken catches up with you, the real work will begin. We know where our weaknesses lie. We know where we have problems with integrity, humility, our creativity, family, and career. Having awareness during periods of transition, to think clearly, and to call on power from other dimensions for guidance toward your unique path, is up to you. But surrendering makes it easier. Your voice will fall upon receiving ears: Corn Woman/*La Virgen* and other spirit beings are only a breath away. Corn Woman's message that a path has been laid out for you is as concrete as a roadmap in hand. Power lies within you; use it. Follow the signposts from your dreams, and you will get there.

C H A P T E R   4

▼

Remembering: Dreaming
Is Reality

The effects of the Christian overlay upon my culture played a huge role in my being unable to sort out the reality of truths that Grandmother revealed to me. The influence of European thought pulled severely on me; I had been brainwashed regarding the "superstitious nature of native cultures."[61] My fundamentalist upbringing had a strong hold on me, even more than I was willing to admit. The following dream illustrates how deeply I yearned to have my perceptions and experiences validated. It occurred about five years into the journals.

Answer

I first met the Creole Woman in the film called "Cat People." Now she is riding in the back seat of our 1950 blue and white Pontiac. Her hair pulled away from her face, covered by a navy blue scarf, and tied at the nape of her neck, accentuates her features. She takes up little space on the right side of the seat.

    "Tell me," I ask of her, "What am I seeing?" I am referring to my dreams and what I really want to know is, "Are my dreams real?"

    She stares back at me with no expression on her face or in her eyes. Her silence conveys the line she used in the movie, "Don't ask questions to answers you already have."

Bear in mind that the old religions of the indigenous cultures are in conflict with current religious beliefs and the Western definition of reality. At points in the exploration of my Christian roots, I even wondered whether yoga was in contradiction to Christian teachings.

Conscious Action within the Dream

Awareness in dreaming is an art that in earlier times was a measure of one's spiritual attainment. And still today, learning to pay attention within your dreams is primary to handling the challenges that arise.

With Corn Woman in the wings, you will need an expanded capacity to receive her enormous gifts. Presence of mind is vital in increasing your consciousness, because her guidance is very specific. She guides her people on their path of transformation, and to expand consciousness, one has to remember her teachings.

Relaxing body and mind lead to the development of heightened dream awareness. You will see that these practices are based on breathing easily. The breath, in turn, increases the awareness of thoughts and feelings in both your waking and dreaming state.

Until now, this dream map has been laying the foundation for understanding the paradigm shift and how the Old Dreamers utilized their dream experiences for transcending duality in their waking world. We have examined the religious beliefs of the old cultures where time and space were sacred, nature was alive with the creative power of the universe, and dreamers lived in a multi-dimensional world.

Now we will work toward the integration of body, mind, and spirit; that integration is essential in the early stages of dreaming. Relaxation of mind and body facilitates this integration through specific practices.

First, let's address a challenge that will arise very quickly—fear. The Old Dreamers knew that in a world of other dimensions and encounters with spirit beings, there is no telling what you will experience and how you will react. If you can withstand the emotions and abject fear that may arise from threatening images—and not run away from them—the dream will open the gates to power and sacred gifts. In reality, these gifts are your divine right. I promise that it will be well worth your time to learn to stay present within the dream when faced with a threat.

So now it's time to take conscious action toward dreaming, and for that you need some preparation. These preparations are interwoven, and there is no right or wrong way of beginning. Integration of body, mind, and spirit will be an ongoing process that will last your entire lifetime. Let's just begin with a straightforward step that is easily attainable—relaxing the body.

Relaxing the Body

The following suggestions will assist in your practice of relaxation. Taking these steps seriously will result in the integration of body, mind, and spirit, a goal that will take a life-time of spiritual practice to fully achieve.

If you have decided to take the suggestions with regard to allowing changes in your waking life as offered in the first chapter, this stage may already seem familiar to you. You may wish to include in your practice slow-movement exercises or lying-down meditations to help you discover where you are holding tension in your body. In the process of letting your body relax, you will find an opening through which long-forgotten memories come to the forefront. You will be amazed at the imprint this can make on your perceptions and feelings.

Kum Nye is a gentle practice of slow movement exercises for releasing tension in the body. The practitioner stretches slowly for forty-five minutes, intermixed with short periods of sitting or lying-down meditation, and allows the body to release tension. This is a two-thousand-year-old Tibetan practice used specifically for integrating body and mind.[62]

Tai chi, chi gong, and yoga are still other effective methods in which a practitioner becomes aware that the patterns she is holding in her body are gradually yielding.

Or you may do a lying down meditation on a soft pad on a flat surface. Your body temperature will drop; so cover yourself with a blanket to keep warm. Observe your breath and the process in which your muscles let go and begin to relax.

As you deepen your practice, you will become aware of stress in your life in general, and will find yourself moving toward a more relaxed approach. The benefits are long-lasting, far-reaching, and highly beneficial for your health and well-being.

Workout sessions at the gym fall short of the desired goal here. We are looking for awareness of tension and how it relates to our thinking and behavior. We slow down our actions, breathe deeply and use only those muscles that are absolutely necessary for movement of one's body.

Relaxing the Mind

If you like, you can begin relaxing the mind by practicing awareness during the day. Keep focused as though in meditation; study the shapes and forms in nature; stand under a tree and examine its bark. Follow its limbs to their farthest reaches, the light filtering through the leaves, its background, the sky. You may notice that it is just as difficult to relax your mind as it is to relax your body. Keep trying. As simple as this little exercise may seem, you will be pleased at the results you will get.

A lying down meditation can be very helpful in keeping your energy up during the day and your mind focused. Let your mind rest, and just observe your thoughts as though they are passing clouds in the sky that will soon be out of sight.

Have a daily practice of meditation. Even five minutes two or three times a day would be very helpful. Just sit quietly, breathe deeply, and observice your thoughts and let them go. You will be amazed at the inventory stored in your mind, and how important it is to let it all go.

Integration

Eventually, practicing relaxation and awareness of body and mind will lead to the integration of mind, body and spirit, where communication flows freely between the three.

Think of your body as a mansion or temple with mysterious places hidden or out of sight. Your body is full of memories that will need healing. Let go and trust yourself.

In your mind, you will find the psychological self that has issues that also need healing. It, too, has its pockets of memories that will present challenges.

Healing at one level facilitates healing of the other.

Dream Yoga

With integration of mind, body, and spirit under way, now we can explore practices toward awareness in dreaming. Various traditions of the East practice dream yoga, wherein the dreamer remains alert to the changes of consciousness while not falling into actual sleep. Practitioners known as yogis (male) and yoginis (female), remain in this state throughout the night.

At the Nyingma Institute, I learned to approach dreams very slowly, as though entering a river of cool rushing water, toe by toe, and let myself gradually adjust to the temperature.

Breathe deeply and follow the sensations in your body that indicate you are relaxing. Especially, follow your thoughts in the same way you would if meditating. You may experience a dream or a fleeting thought. Notice it, and come back to breath.

If you choose to remain conscious throughout the night, place a pillow on your stomach so that you don't roll over and fall asleep. Focus on your breath pushing the pillow up and down as you inhale and exhale. Take all the time you need to become adjusted. It is impossible to rush the process. Observe the deeper states of consciousness. Be gentle with yourself, and if you need to sleep, so be it.

The desire to practice dream yoga may be a good reason for you to join a meditation group. Be sure to surround yourself with support, and keep in mind that these are the early steps that will expand your awareness of details in your personal life. The flow of your mind will carry you into worlds you didn't know existed. Trust the process, and take it slowly.

My Early Dream Journals

Here is what I experienced as my inner and outer worlds began to merge through meditation and relaxation.

In 1980, my brother John gave me a set of books, *A Course in Miracles,*[63] comprised of a manual, text, and daily lessons for the year. The course teaches that there are only two emotions: love and fear. The lessons can be practiced at one's own pace for as long as one desires. This practice helped me realize that, instead of events in the world being consistent for everyone, what I construe to be my reality are the contents of my thoughts. Over the years, I have practiced the lessons repeatedly and, with it, continue to change my perception of the world and my interaction.

I also did the Autogenic Training exercises three times a day by letting my spine collapse while sitting up. I visualized bringing heat into my limbs, and closed the exercise with a phrase such as, "I am at peace." I also practiced these exercises lying down. Through Autogenic Training, I learned to relax my body muscle group by muscle group until I could relax entirely through awareness of my breath. With this practice alone, I began to remember the first day in my first foster home. Each time my shoulders relaxed, the image would come back.

Subsequently, I became a volunteer at the Center for Attitudinal Healing and combined the work with my internship in a graduate program at San Francisco State University. The principles of the Center for Attitudinal Healing were developed by Jerry Jampolsky, MD, and are also based on *The Course in Miracles*:

1. The essence of our being is love.

2. Health is inner peace. Healing is letting go of fear.

3. Giving and receiving are the same.

4. We can let go of the past and the future.

5. Now is the only time there is, and each instant is for giving.

6. We can learn to love others and ourselves by forgiving rather than judging.

7. We can become love finders rather than faultfinders.

8. We can choose and direct ourselves to be peaceful inside regardless of what is happening outside.

9. We are students and teachers to each other.

10. We can focus on the whole of life rather than the fragments.

11. Since love is eternal, death need not be viewed as fearful.

12. We can always perceive others and ourselves as either extending love or as giving a call for help.[64]

I went with the objective to learn about love, and discovered how little I knew about it. I also learned how skilled I was against getting close to people. Regardless, this teaching worked and helped me open up to new types of relationships. I took some risks, and my heart opened to families that had loved ones with life-threatening illnesses.

With the *Course In Miracles*, The Principles of Attitudinal Healing, the training in my graduate program, and the teachings at the Nyingma Institute, my perceptions and thought processes changed dramatically. These activities brought me closer to understanding my inner process and facilitated the expansion of awareness; yet, the hard lessons came later.

I thought I was doing fine, but beneath the surface, there was a rumble of which I was yet unaware. I was acutely sensitive to the stress and tension stored in my body. I could sense it with the first morning stretches. But by the time I had written down the dreams and done the yoga, I was in a completely different frame of mind and ready for the day, but this seeming ease covered the underlying *un*ease.

Something was deeply disturbing me. I didn't realize how intensely these practices were impacting my reality. It took time, but eventually it became evident that my internal world was undergoing a total renovation. The years of emotional and spiritual neglect when my mother worked, lay heavy across my shoulders. It seemed as though I was encased in a block of ice from my neck down to the middle of my thighs. Years passed before my body completely rested.

As I forewarned, the journey inward is an arduous undertaking—I speak from hard-won experience. The integration of mind, body, and spirit evolves slowly. I continue to fluctuate between releasing tension and taking control, though not to the same extremes.

With the integration of mind and body coming together, now we are ready to explore how dreamtime awareness can develop.

Learning to be conscious in dreaming is part of the task of learning to navigate in other dimensions. In the "I Am Where I Am" dream (1977), I am discovering my ability to think and make decisions. The feeling in the dream is as clear and vivid as if I had been awake. I am also remembering the waking state and the fact that I am dreaming.

I Am Where I Am

> *The sensation of being weightless and finding myself high off the ground amidst the branches of a tree frightens me. I remember my reading from the waking state on the various precepts of other realities.*
>
> *As I recall this information in the dream, I realize that my discomfort is natural. Feeling the fear, I inhale and exhale deeply. The floating continues, and my attention goes to a branch higher up the tree. I notice that it is my attention that is taking me there. I pretend to be like Alice in Wonderland observing the changes; it seems as though a movie has been set in motion, and floating is the most natural and wonderful thing to do.*

The "reading from the waking state" refers to one of the Seth books by Jane Roberts.[65] The dream occurred about a year after beginning the dream journal. Once I realized I could control the floating sensations, it felt as normal as the thinking process in deciding what to cook for dinner—it seemed that commonplace. Until the time I realized I could shift my attention to another part of the tree, I was immersed in fear.

Eventually, with your stress reduction/meditation practice, you will realize that attention in your dreams is vital and possible. The "Don't Lose Your Head" dream specifically illustrated that point for me. Gradually, I was connecting the two dimensions, but I was not totally aware that the two could be related.

Don't Lose Your Head

Strolling through the arboretum in San Francisco, I come upon two monks sitting on a green park bench amidst the ferns and elephant plants. One nods off, and his head rolls down his shoulders and settles on the bench; the other, sitting casually with his arms stretched across the back of the bench, is near an outright burst of laughter. Winking, he looks at me directly as though to say, "Isn't he ridiculous? He goes to sleep and loses his head."

With a sense of humor, my inner teacher, the monk, showed me the essence of remaining aware of my thoughts in dreams as in waking meditation.

Flying

Some dreamers have reported no fear in learning how to fly. Because the laws of physics are different in the dream state, learning to fly in dreams and being conscious may cause some trepidation. Flying is part of multidimensional travel.

From the following dream, we learn that it is possible to learn from dream lessons on flying. A few months after becoming aware of my ability to act within the dream, I had the following three dreams: "Lesson from My Father," "Lesson from Mama," and "Getting It."

In the "Lesson from My Father" dream, I experience outright terror as I begin to take flight.

Lesson from My Father

At the end of the bus line, I get off the bus with my father and a group of people, and proceed toward the stairs that link Vallejo and Broadway at Lyon in San Francisco. The stairs are so steep that they necessitate our walking down backward. A heavyset black woman goes ahead of me. I watch carefully where she places her feet as she makes it to the bottom with blithe easy steps.

When my turn comes, fear grips and paralyzes me. My father, who is right behind in line, pushes me to get me going, but I get stuck on the first rung of what has now become a ladder. His push takes me off guard, and I lose my balance. I begin yelling for help, but it's too late; I am too far from the top of the ladder for anyone to extend a hand, and too high up from the bottom for anyone to reach me. People stand by helplessly watching my predicament.

I shriek in terror as I sail through the air with my arms and legs frozen in an extended position like a wooden horse. A Native American man flies up to me from below to assist me and puts a tight hold around my waist. I feel safe and relax with his control over my flight, and we alight gently on the ground. As he lets go of me, he smiles warmly, and his spirit feels gentle and kind.

As you can see from the fear that "grips and paralyzes me" and the fact that "I shriek in terror as I sail through the air," this dream is marked by the absence of awareness that I could control my trajectory by directing my consciousness. Of course, progress does not occur in a straight line, just as it doesn't necessarily follow a straight line in waking life. But, a spirit being arrives to offer unconditional love and support.

The following dream seems to take on a different tenor with the element of safety afforded by the ceiling of the gymnasium. The lesson is very simple and completely threat-free to me, even though I have not yet learned to fly.

Lesson from Mamá

Just go like this," Mamá prompts me, making a smooth infinity sign with a baton. We stand in the opaque light filtering through the frosted windows of a gymnasium. I take a running start and jump on one foot as though ready to spring off a diving board. The ample space to practice flying creates safety for me, because I am wobbly and apt to fly off into space, noticed by my bumping on the ceiling. I keep practicing until I learn to control my flight.

In the "Lesson from Mamá" dream, she is giving me specific instructions as to what I should do in flight. "Just go like this," she instructs me. Bumping my head along the ceiling shows I lacked skill and control, but the ceiling acts as a container to manage this task.

I find the progression of the lessons interesting in that they take my safety into consideration. In "Lesson from My Father," my father just shoved me off, I shrieked as I sailed through the air, and help arrived from a Native American man. In contrast, I'm protected by the structure of the gymnasium in "Lesson from Mamá."

In the third dream, "Getting It," my ability is tested once again by an elder who reaches for my arm to maintain my trajectory. These three elders played a vital role in the lessons as they unfolded over the years. "Lessons from my Father" and "Lessons from Mamá" were just a couple of weeks apart. "Getting It" occurred about a year later.

Getting It

The skies are blue, crisp, and wide open. I stand on a lush green knoll with three elders who are wearing heavy, long, army-green coats. My task is to learn to make the infinity sign with precision. But, like a helium balloon, I keep drifting into space. One of the elders grabs for my arm and begins guiding my trajectory. Instead of a mere arm's length to practice, he grows as tall as a redwood.

Up, up, and around I go as he makes the wide sweeping motions, until my course becomes steady. Soon, he lets go. I swoop upwards and down with an acute thrill and sense of expansion; then low, my nose almost scraping the ground; and I am flying with the control of a skilled apprentice.

In "Getting It," the open space is minimized by the presence of the elder who guides my flight. What characterizes this dream is my success in flying solo and the thrill of flying itself. Thereafter, because fear brought me to attention, I had no trouble flying. Later, I learned to *initiate* the flying.

"Getting It" also features the group of elders who play a role in the journals since their early stages. I was curious to know who these Native American "guys" were. But whoever they were, their appearance was another confirmation that I had entered a paradigm in which spirit beings were coming to my aid. They felt like teachers unconditional and compassionate.

In "The Test" dream, I begin to have more control and have developed the ability to withstand fear and to make decisions within the dream. I had this dream about two years after the previous three dreams.

The Test

Another test. This time, I stand behind a thick plate glass, thinking that I am stumped. Fear grips me as I try to penetrate the thickness of the glass.

"Project through it," I tell myself.

I position my feet and steady my mind. With the force of a space shuttle, I make it to the other side of the glass. Immediately, heavy electrical wires confront me. For a moment I hesitate, then make a split-second decision to fly through and risk possible annihilation.

With my having gone through these obstacles, the element of risk lifts. I relax and slow down.

Treading air above a wooded area, I see a learning center below me. A class is gathering in a shaded amphitheater. I fly down to have a closer look and slow down even further to select a place to sit. I touch ground and sit next to a student I apparently know.

"The Test" dream seems to be marked by greater ease of traveling in other dimensions. Initially, I felt "stumped" but was able to recognize that I could travel through the "plate glass." Then I tested the situation by going through "heavy electrical wires" and "risk possible annihilation." I made several decisions in this dream: first to go through the plate glass; then, the heavy electrical wires; then, to join a class, slow down my flight a first and second time, and finally select a place to sit. "The Test" dream took place almost eight years after the inception of the journals. Eventually, I even learned to play in space.

Summary

The early stages of dreaming involve becoming acquainted with our inner terrain, feelings, and tension. Letting our bodies and minds relax, integrating mind body and spirit, and developing awareness in the dream—these are the tasks to master in the early stages of dreaming. The lessons will vary, but with time you will decipher the direction and meaning of your dreams. As much as possible, be sensitive to your inner prompting, and interweave the suggestions from the first chapter. Gaining attention and awareness is a slow process, and the emotions that arise may be challenging. Be patient and stay connected to a community or spiritual director for support.

Learning to travel in other dimensions involves as much attention and practice as one would put into becoming a skilled artist, dancer, actor, writer, or a musician. It doesn't "just happen." When we pay attention in the waking state by meditating and doing exercises in relaxation or quiet observation of nature, we can begin to see that awakening within the dream can occur easily and effortlessly. Be alert within the dream, and pay attention while awake. You have plunged into an ocean, and the waters are bound to get murky. Determination is the key. You will discover magnificent spirit beings that will come to your aid.

And now we come back to the supreme reason for delving into the depths of awareness. In the softening of your grip over mind, body, and spirit, you will begin to remember Corn Woman's essence. Snippets of a broader horizon and a greater reality will come to your attention. With the mirror of truth now before you for the first time, you see yourself as you genuinely are; never again will you believe that you are that small being you once thought was real. Your connection to a greater truth becomes too significant to deny, for you have entered the paradigm of the Old Dreamers and Corn Woman's path toward transformation. Through stillness and a new, keen sense of observation, you will triumph. Your journey home is established.

The "Wheel of Life" dream that follows embodies the vastness I encountered. Though it's a dream where I faced death, I saw in it the space beyond, a spectacular reality. I made the decision to stay with the feeling of drowning and to accept death. The Symphony took me beyond ecstasy. I didn't record this dream in story form; instead, the account rose from within as a poem.

Wheel of Life

I stand at the edge of a cliff.
Mother Earth begins to tremble.
I shake.
The earth beneath my feet shakes and gives way
To the Blue Pacific below.
Down, down I go, like a child on a slide,
Into the waiting arms of Mother Ocean.

Down
Down
Down
Down
Past the last breath.
I drink in death and
Darkness surrounds me.

I wait
Wait
And wait
Until I hear celestial music.
A symphony,
A wondrous symphony.
Everything in the Universe resonates with this
Marvelous song;
Such joy,
Such freedom,
Perfection in rhythm and tone.

Nothing, absolutely nothing, exists
Beyond its reach.

Down I go
Then, like Jonah delivered by the whale,
I, too, am deposited
Onto a sunny beach,
A community by the sea.
My home is a small white cottage with yellow trim,
Circled by a white picket fence with a
Wheel of Life for a gate.

CHAPTER 5

▼

Encounters with Spirit Beings: Shift in Paradigm

It was a hot, balmy summer night in 1958. I remember, because the house was wide-open—the front door, all the windows, including the ones in my bedroom—and the lights in the kitchen and dining room were on. I was fifteen years old, and I still recall the stillness of the night. I had just finished washing my hair and had the towel wrapped around my head. My mother was taking a shower, and we were the only ones home. I took the towel off and leaned over to let my hair fall loose and to brush the tangles out. I had recently gotten a perm and was not used to its new length. I was casually measuring it, and it almost went down to the floor. I stood in front of the art deco dresser with its big round mirror, studying my hair out of the corner of my eye.

Just then, I heard a car pull up to the grove of olive trees next to our property line; someone got out, and the car door slammed shut. I thought it odd that someone would be using the grove; the front door was open and no one used the shortcut to the backdoor anymore. I stopped to listen to the footsteps that seemed to be coming toward me. I was transfixed. The crunch of the leaves told me that indeed they were actually coming in my direction.

"Chepe, Chepe," I heard my brother Gilbert's voice calling. I remained silent. The steps retreated back through the grove of trees, to the car, and once again, I heard the car door shut. I felt a chill run down my spine as I took three quick steps to look. I had a clear view, and there was no car—only an eerie silence in the half-lit street.

"Did you hear a car drive up?" my mother asked in Spanish as she came out of the shower.

"Si," I answered, making no other comment.

"And Gilbert's voice?" she continued.

"*Si, si,*" I answered in the affirmative, adding nothing more.

She thought for a moment.

"I think he's on his way here," she concluded.

Things like that often happened when she and I were home alone, so when she offered her interpretation, I took it at face value. We both went to bed that night expecting to hear something of my brother. Gilbert was stationed in Riverside in Southern California, and every now and then he would surprise us with a visit, but it had been months since he had phoned or written. Around two o'clock in the morning, the telephone rang.

"Come pick me up. I'm in Modesto," he said.

Gilbert had hitchhiked, and his ride ended thirty miles south of Stockton on Highway 99 at the all-night truck stop.

Paraadigm

As a *curandera*, you know that the Mexican culture is naturally abundant in stories of spirits appearing and leaving messages of one kind or another, or events occurring out of sync with space and time. Yet, the fact that the Chicana culture has been twice colonized, and has over time lost its reference points, due to the widespread influence of the Western worldview, many doubt the validity of these stories.[66] But you as a *curandera* must acknowledge and validate this ancient reality, for that is the paradigm in which the Old Dreamers and cultures navigated. This applies especially to Western medicine women, mystics, and artists who—in spite of the pull they feel from their own old culture—are heavily influenced by scientific thought.

Spirit beings visiting us from other dimensions appear in our dreams and wak-ing life like strands of golden light or forms of energy, but most commonly, as beings who look just like you and me. When they come, they impart wisdom that can ultimately aid you in your path toward transformation. Their messages can be for your personal development as well as for the perpetuation of the ancient culture in general.

In my study, I found the blending of dimensions commonplace. *The Chroni-cles of Michoacan*[67] shows how ordinary these encounters were for indigenous people prior to the conquest. People lived side-by-side with the departed, and spirits appeared to them to give information or make requests. For example, a young man dreamed that a woman came to him and touched him on the shoul-der, showing him the disarray of her clothes and the condition of the feathers on her back. And then she requested that a temple be built in her honor on that very location.

> Awaken, *Tangaxoan*. Why do you say you are an orphan, yet you sleep? Awaken, look, I am *Xaratangan*; go ahead and clear the way to where I am to be. Go look at the foot of this mountain where the brambles are thickest and you will find there the seat of my temple. That is my house called the house of Parrot Feathers and the House of Chicken Feathers. Look to the right where the ball game will be; there I must feed the gods at midday, and you will see the site of my baths ... take care to renew my adornments and you shall be favored, for I shall make your house and your granaries, and they shall be filled with food.[68]

As the story unfolds in *The Chronicles,* the father of the dreamer identifies Xaratangan, and admonishes the young man of the reality of the dream. "Most fortunate one ... That woman you mention is not an old woman, but rather the goddess Xaratanga ... Go clear her temples and her throne and place incense there, make fires and smoke in that place, for she will smell them when she comes."[69]

In this story, the goddess has blessed the youth and made a request of him. First, she is touching him on the shoulder, calling him by his name and referring to an important image he has of himself. "Awaken, Tangaxoan, why do you say you are an orphan, yet you sleep? Awaken, look, I am Xaratanga ..." Xaratanga is calling the young man to attention—"awaken"—and to recognize his own uniqueness, also that he is not alone and that there is another world. The spirit being is admonishing him to take stock of his life and is giving him an opportu-nity to meet his destiny. In building a temple for her, he "shall be favored, for I shall make your house and your granaries, and they shall be filled with food." The exchange between the dreamer and the spirit being has a sense of immediacy and reality to those who listen to the telling of the dream.

It's wise to heed these interactions with respect. They will inspire and encourage you as though the advice or information is coming from a valued family member who is intimate with the most personal aspects of your life.

Grandmother First Appears

Over the years, I, too, continued to feel that same kind of interactive reality that had once caused me great bewilderment. About a year into the journals (1977), I had a dream in which Grandmother appeared for the first time, inviting herself on my journey. An elder, she spoke Spanish, and befriended me in a most gracious, compassionate manner. She was Aztec, Mayan, or other Native American—her gray hair was in braids, her hips broad, and she was anchored to the earth. Hearing Spanish in my dreams was uncommon since I no longer spoke Spanish as often as before my mother's death. On the surface, my life looked like any other culturally assimilated life, but in my dreams, Grandmother was waiting for me; waiting to begin the training.

Abuelita
(Grandmother)

On a warm afternoon I float on my back in the calm, safe waters of Baby Beach on the Island of Maui, studying the soft white clouds contrasting on the infinity of the pale blue sky. I get out of the water and walk toward my things on the beach, and pick up a plain white towel to dry myself off.

An older Mexican-Indian woman walks up to me and simply asks, "¿Voy contigo?" (Shall I join you?) This was new, my noticing race and language. I instinctively see that I "know" her. Her eyes sparkle, her smile teases me—but I can't quite place her. I rummage through my memory trying to remember, but come up with no stepping-stone to affirm the feelings.

Nonetheless, I sense a bond between us, and I immediately trust her. Without knowing where we are going, I accept her offer to join me.

"Sí, cómo no." I answer, casually drying my hair with the sandy towel. Yes, of course.

"¿Voy contigo?" It seemed so natural to have her join me. Little did I know that in Grandmother's invitation to accept her as my gentle guide and teacher, I would discover the Shaper and Former. Revealing the secrets of my indigenous past, she, the dream-giver—with whispers, dancing eyes, and dazzling smile—

humored me. She cajoled and tricked me into dreaming. She turned my world inside out so that it gradually became obvious to me that I was actually "asleep" while awake, and "awake" while asleep.

Grandmother appeared to me in a number of ways in my dreams beginning in 1977, bringing out the memory of *La Virgen de Guadalupe*. Her appearance this side of reality left a remarkable imprint upon my consciousness. Her radiant vivaciousness always brought me to attention within dreams. Lessons she imparted were beyond my earthly understanding, always had purpose, and were related to my increased understanding of reality. Her presence gave me the sense she was particularly important to my mission in life. Aside from her unconditional love and acceptance of me, there was something greater that I found.

I soon became aware that she was teaching a point of view vastly different from the one I knew. With the following dream, her teachings began to reconfigure my sense of the structure of the universe and gradually brought me to recognize the feminine face of God. In my dreamscape, an insight would flash across my mind, and later, in the morning, as I examined and re-experienced the dream, the insight would expand under the gaze of the pen, and take on a life of its own. "*La Diferencia*" illustrates this point. I had this dream in 1984, during my years in graduate school and at the Nyingma Institute.

La Diferencia

Again, darkness surrounds me and I drift like a feather in space. I feel the presence behind me. Grandmother instructs me to recognize my ability to receive this important information that comes to me in sensations, not in words:

"Though there are no comparisons, some teachings are best for men only, and some for women only."

The feminine sensations flutter in my womb.

The "feminine sensations" jarred my memory of something familiar, and as I juxtaposed it against other dreams revealing feminine energy, it came into focus. It felt like a shakedown in which my normal view of life was being uprooted, dusted off, reshaped, and returned to me.

She Comes While I'm Awake

I will always remember the day Grandmother first appeared to me in my waking life. The day began like any other day. I got up early, was in class at San Francisco State University by eight o'clock in the morning, returned home at noon, and had lunch. I was forty-one years old. This was eight years into the journals. At this point in time, I was practicing meditation and kum nye, the ancient Tibetan slow movement practice referred to in the previous chapter, and doing the internship for the graduate program at the Center for Attitudinal Healing that was then in Tiburon. At San Francisco State University, I was also learning about biofeedback and measuring the relaxation response with biofeedback instruments while I practiced the Autogenic Training exercises.

After lunch, I made my preparations for going into a lying-down meditation, laying out a mat, and beige wool blanket. I looked at the watch beside me, and saw that it was one o'clock. At four, I needed to leave from Third Avenue and Parnassus for the ferry downtown to get me to The Center in Tiburon by six. I was alone in the house, I had plenty of time, and I made the suggestion to myself that I come out of meditation in forty-five minutes.

Background information is vital here. Just prior to my story, I had participated in a retreat, and the issue of women ringing the gong for early morning practice and meditation had come up. The women felt some agitation and were dissatisfied with the explanation that "women's energy is different, and therefore, they should not ring the bell." In the days that followed, I thought about the debates and could still hear the dean of the institute saying, "Why are you assuming that it means something 'bad' or 'wrong' about women?" I myself hadn't come to a conclusion about the bell ringing.

Meditation

I closed my eyes, and went deeply into relaxation, maintaining awareness of my breath and body relaxing. At the agreed upon time, I heard footsteps coming from the kitchen—soft footsteps of someone walking barefoot. I remembered the story I had heard of the monk who walked on sand and left no footprint, and walked on stone and left an indentation; that's what these footsteps sounded like to me. I opened my eyes, and turned my head to see who was there.

By this time, she was so close that I could see the coffee-brown and the lines of time on the heels of her feet. She stood midway, near my waist, and—my eyes following up her body—I could see her clearly.

She was a heavyset Indian grandmother with gray hair and high cheekbones. Her smile conveyed an acknowledgment from beyond space and time.

In the instant our eyes met, I was more than my forty years and the psychological self I knew at that time; with her, I was ageless, wise, and infinite. She knew me completely, and I felt that the expanse of my being was as far-reaching as the edges of the universe. We were One and the same.

Smiling, she clapped her hands three times, and projected the thought, "Do you get it?"

Her hands resting at her side, she continued her tender gaze upon me, filling my being with her love and compassion.

She was referring, of course, to masculine and feminine energy and the vast difference between the two. In that split second, I understood what "feminine" meant. I experienced it as a creative force reaching into infinity. La Virgen's belt around her abdomen is a symbol of the creative process in embryo—nurturing, embracing, knowing.[70] Sensations of lightness and great joy rippled through me, and for an instant, my body disappeared and I was pure energy.

Her mission accomplished, she walked toward the kitchen again, and I followed her with my eyes. I wanted to run and catch her and hold her as long as I could, but I knew where she was going, and that I could not.

She disappeared before my eyes. Once she was out of sight, I could move. I ran quickly into the kitchen where she had exited, hoping ... The stove was cold; everything was as it had been. I kept looking for that crack in space that would lead me to her. I was convinced that somewhere between the Wedgwood and the stucco wall, I would find a subtle line that would take me to her world."

I felt infused with a current that gracefully flowed from her into my entire being. I felt her greatness, and in her presence, I recognized my oneness with her.

It was through this meeting that I finally came to know the importance of feminine energy and the vital part it plays in the balance of the universe. In contrast to the spacious feminine energy I was feeling, the sound of metal felt cold and hard. Still, her presence was a mystery to me that I did not discuss with anyone until I started working on the first manuscript ten years later.

Today I look back on the highlight of that experience and realize that she touched my consciousness and brought me one step closer to remembering the message of Corn Woman. Through the days that followed, I knew something had changed, but gradually the memory of the experience faded into the background of my life. Nonetheless, my consciousness shifted, and I continued to have other shifts in consciousness that anchored me to this experience.

"Grandmother Dances" is another dream that illustrates how she continued to impact my life. This dream occurred within the six-month period during which Grandmother visited me. I continued my practice of yoga and meditated several hours each day; this included doing the kum nye relaxation exercises. The significance of this dream was the redefinition of currents of energy in the body as I was experiencing them in yoga and kum nye. Those currents related to the integration of mind, body, and spirit. I saw that there was an obvious overlap between the teachings at the Nyingma Institute, and those in my dreams.

Grandmother Dances

I sit toward the back of a classroom waiting for our instructor. Most of the students sit toward the front in animated discussion. Grandmother walks in and announces class will now begin. A young white man raises his hand and immediately asks for a demonstration of dancing from Grandmother. I wince and think how irregular this is—to be asking Grandmother to dance—a great disrespect to our Teacher. She reads my thoughts, winks at me, and starts dancing.

Her dancing prompts in me a heightened ability to see, as though I suddenly have x-ray vision. I discern different levels of her teaching, and I become attuned to a heightened sense of consciousness.

On the surface, she is merely going back and forth several steps, bending back-wards, kicking her legs high up, and she does this with so much freedom in body and spirit. The class goes wild with exhilaration, clapping and screaming like kids at a Beatles concert. This just adds juice to her demonstration, and brings out her playfulness and sense of humor as she kicks her legs up higher and higher.

Another level of the lesson is on 'resilience.' The body needs the resilience, the strength to accomplish its tasks in the material plane. Resilience also serves to supply energy in accomplishing the tasks from the material to the spiritual plane, and vice versa. Resilience is the connector that, when plugged into the outlet of the universe, permits the successful flow of energy.

Resilience is also important in mastering the different levels of consciousness we travel through. Without resilience, our energy withers and we become brittle. With resilience, we also allow our consciousness to go into unfamiliar territory.

I realize that Grandmother's movements are stretching my own limitations of consciousness as though my mind is like an artist's canvas being pulled over a frame.

When she concludes her demonstration, she stands behind the podium, smiling calmly, delighted to have this opportunity to perform, and delighted that we have "gotten" the teaching.

This dream, in particular, also impacted my sense of time and space. Again, my consciousness expanded, and I became one with the grandeur of eternity. Travel into other realms cannot be ignored, nor can one's worldview remain static. In Grandmother's dancing, I found explanations for the spiritual teachings I was receiving at the Nyingma Institute and the Center for Attitudinal Healing. I continued in an upward spiral. It was as though I had been thrown into a vibrator, my brain cells being shaken free of their memories and reconfigured to incorporate the emerging new worldview. I got a glimpse of the meaning of kundalini—the serpent energy of the spine that awakens through Yogic practices—that I had read about. Seeing Grandmother's agility, I recognized the need for fluency, and it inspired me to keep at my efforts to integrate mind, body, and spirit.

Time and Space

With the spiritual remaking through Grandmother's presence, I also learned about other facets of reality. In one of the lessons I received from her, she showed me about time and space being sacred and imbued with power. Awareness of this sacredness required my waking and sleeping attention.

Power Spots

"See those dark blue spots down there?" Grandmother indicates, pointing her brown finger to two large spots on the ground that from where we hover above the earth look like deep indigo concentrations of swirling energy in northern Mexico. I marvel at the beauty of the color, aware of the emanations of energy from them, but mostly, I am keenly aware of being in the presence of a sacred being and feel protected, as though being cradled by the mother of the universe. We fly down together, and as we draw closer, the indigo spots seem to fade into the terrain of brown earth with nothing to mark their uniqueness. We continue flying south, alight in a woodsy area near Guanajuato, and join a group of people in conversation on a Sunday afternoon. I study them closely to see whether they notice anything peculiar about us. They open the circle to include us with no interruption or sign of anything unusual happening.

As I studied them in the dream, the "dark blue spots" emanated wonderful sensations of beauty and harmony. Whether I looked at the spots or marveled at Grandmother's remarkable loveliness, I was keenly aware of her presence and the magnificence she was imparting to me.

Entering the dreams in the journals, I found much difficulty, not only in describing the ecstasy I had experienced in her presence, but also in defining what I was being shown. I had no cultural traditions to support my new perception of reality. Even when Grandmother appeared to me, I found it difficult to explain the appearance's significance.

A Huge Shift

Among other things, she shifted my perception from a monotheistic god to a dual gender god and reshaped my structure of the universe. The spots of energy Grandmother pointed out were crucial in explaining many other lessons, particularly about time, power, and destiny. Something in her pointing alerted me to the pervasive Now. I began to see where integration of mind, body, and spirit had its place in my life and spiritual growth. Just as in meditation I became aware of the contents of my thoughts, I also became aware of where I put my attention—period.

Over the years, I came to cherish my relationship with Grandmother. Her appearance evoked deep emotion, compassion, and an awareness of my spiritual nature that no human agency could have duplicated.

Summary

So, let me affirm your experiences and encounters with spirit beings. Validating these experiences necessitates acknowledgment of the paradigm of the old cultures. These are the stories that abound in the Chicana culture. In my study, I found that encounters with Spirit beings were accepted as purposeful reality in the old cultures, not as random meetings, and were not regarded in any respect as hallucinations. Interactions with spirit beings carried specific lessons and purposes. Today, they still serve the same purpose—to shed light on our spiritual journeys and pass on information and messages. They inform us of the wisdom of our ancestors and the way they saw reality. Meetings and interchanges with spirit beings are intentional and deliberate—not only for learning to travel and understand other realms. They also aid in expanding our consciousness, which serves to empower us in manifesting our destiny and creativity. Ultimately, that expansion of awareness leads us to our true identity, and to playing out our role as participants in the return and perpetuation of the old culture.

Modern-day thinking influences dreamers. Western thought today frequently invalidates multidimensionality. In linear thinking, we ignore events of these kinds because they are outside the realm of accepted reality. But as a dreamer/*curandera*, it is important that you validate all your experiences and the empowerment that comes from these special encounters with spirit beings.

Without validation of our expanded consciousness, we are no different than Tangaxoan going through life believing he is an orphan.

Make no mistake about it; *consciousness is spiritual currency, vital and vibrant, to be used for the supreme good of the world.* The inspiration may come as subtly as a subliminal message embedded in a movie, flashing before one's eyes so quickly that it does not register with the conscious mind. But take note of what you see, and bring it forth into this dimension.

Most important, it's playing out your role as a *curandera*/artist/healer that will strengthen your reconnection to Corn Woman; this far surpasses any other responsibility or obligation you may ever know. In that role, you are laying the foundation for your own transformation. It takes faith.

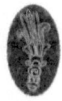

CHAPTER 6

▼

Destiny Beckons

Destiny hit me like a sledgehammer with my mother's death in 1962. The years of disrupted family life created by her working outside the home had taken their toll on our relationship. The summer she died was my first year after high school graduation. Due to her medical condition, she was no longer working, and I had thought the family would be together again. Instead, she left for Los Angeles to help my brother who was having a marital crisis. No one in our family stopped her from leaving, and a few months later, she came back in an ambulance to spend the remainder of her time at home. I was furious at her for shattering my dream. At eighteen, I wasn't thinking of death, and in my youth, I wasn't heeding the signposts that foretold my mother's imminent passing. Little did I know that my fate was being sealed, that I was now to roam through life like a lone wolverine.

A few days after her return, I was sitting at the kitchen table by myself when I heard the shifting of her slippers slowly coming toward me through the dining room. I could hear her labored, shallow breathing, and I wondered whether I should lend a hand and ask her to lean on me. But I couldn't move. It felt hypocritical to offer assistance without asking forgiveness for having given her the cold shoulder since her return.

Mamá finally got to the table and sat across from me. I could feel her eyes waiting to catch mine, but being stubborn and proving my point seemed more important than calling a truce, so I held my eyes fixed on my half-empty plate of rice, beans, and fried chicken. I wanted to blast her, "How could you leave us when you didn't have to?" My skills in communication were nonverbal and I gave her a sneer of total disdain and disgust, then turned away. She asked me a couple of questions, and I answered, "Si," and "No."

About nine o'clock that evening she called me from her bedroom. "Noni, please bring me a hot washcloth."

I ran to the room and saw that she was having another heart attack and gasping for air. Frightened, I grabbed a washcloth, dipped it into the running water without letting it heat up, thinking there wasn't enough time. I handed her the cold, twisted, wet cloth, and watched her apply it to her heart area. I held the tears back, my heart aching, and though I wanted to hold her lovingly, I stood there frozen and suspended in space. She continued to gasp. When my brother Chepe, the youngest of the boys, came home at nine thirty, he called the hospital and an ambulance came for her.

The next night, June 29, 1962, my brothers, father, and I stood motionless around her bedside at St. Joseph's Hospital in Stockton. Her arms rested on the white bed linens, and I moved in closer to her. She had survived several cardiac arrests the previous year, and I was sure she was invincible and would pull through once more.

I looked at her tired face, her hands resting softly, and I remembered my disrespect the previous day. Once more, I was paralyzed with confusion. I stood there for what seemed like an eternity. Then very slowly, with the jerky movements of a crane, I reached mechanically toward her hand. I could not forgive myself that we had become strangers to one another. Maybe we had once laughed and danced together, but I couldn't remember whether I had dreamed that or it had actually happened. Now, all that felt real was the estrangement and wide gap between us. The memories of arguments and fights came flooding before my eyes until my hand dropped on hers; and, ever so subtly, she relaxed and breathed her last breath.

In the months that followed, I tried to live in our family home, but the emptiness without my mother was unbearable, and I transferred with the telephone company to San Francisco. A couple of years later, my father picked up his life and, helter-skelter, sold the house we had lived in since 1948, remarried, and settled in San Diego.

Away from my culture, I was exposed to experiences I wasn't prepared to handle; I got involved with an inappropriate man who broke my heart, and then moved back to Stockton to live with my oldest brother while I went to secretarial school.

Upon graduation from secretarial school at twenty-one, I again left the community that had rejected me, and came back to San Francisco. I could not stay home and pretend that it was otherwise.

El Destino

With hindsight, I can see much more about my life than I could then. I learned, as the years passed, that the pain from my mother's death, loss of home, and loss of culture, actually provided the fertile ground in which I was to cultivate my real purpose.

According to the old traditions, I could not have escaped those events, and the events themselves set the stage for my destiny to be fulfilled. They created the turns in the road to lead me in certain directions.

El Destino is an expression used in the Mexican culture to describe a strong belief that things determined by God are best left to stand alone—without judgment or complaint. In my research, I found a connection from the past to this belief. The Aztec and Maya believed that the God of Duality determined peoples' fate. The *Popol Vuh* tells us in the Creation Stories:

> It was said that in the twelfth heaven
> Our fates were determined.
> When the child is placed in the womb,
> His fate comes to him there,
> It is sent to him by the Lord of Duality.[71]

Castaneda recounted a lesson imparted to him by his teacher, Don Juan, a Yaqui dreamer, in describing the power of destiny. They were hiking along a steep ravine when Castaneda stopped to tie his shoelaces. Those few moments of rest saved them from a boulder that then rolled down the mountain. Castaneda wrote, "The size of the boulder made its fall a very impressive event ... Don Juan said that the force that rules our destinies is outside of ourselves and has nothing to do with our acts or volition. Sometimes that force would make us stop walking on our way and bend over to tie our shoelaces, as I had just done."[72] But, on another day, that same force could do the same thing and arrange our destruction without warning.

For the dreamer/*curandera,* the topic of destiny is especially important because it defines her role in life, a role that is transmitted through dreams. The Aztec and Mayan cultures highly valued the process of discovering one's destiny, because the path toward it ran parallel to the path toward transformation. The dream guides the dreamer by showing the next level of attainment. As our dreams direct us, we find that in deciphering our destinies, we enter upon the ultimate of spiritual tasks—discovery of sacred gifts that lead to transformation and transcendence.

Belief in destiny is a difficult concept for Westerners to accept because the idea is in direct opposition to self-determination by the individual. Yet, destiny neither negates responsibility nor leaves us open to whim. We have many choices to make. *La curandera*/medicine woman/artist may recognize a special talent in healing, music, art, writing, or dancing. The list is endless. In this paradigm, developing these talents requires taking personal responsibility to develop them for the sake of the culture. Destiny gives the means by which to create the powerful symbols and teachings resulting from art. When destiny speaks, we feel the expansion of consciousness. The empowerment that follows provides the certainty and wherewithal to follow through.

Discovering our destiny is a complex process, because we become privy to the immensity of the universe. We see this in the example of "*El Poder de la Montaña*" (Power of the Mountain) dream that follows in this chapter. Yet, a feeling stemming from a deep knowing *can* be coupled with a doubt that dwarfs the gift and leaves you hungering for more proof of the greatness of what is given. Faith is indispensable; patience, crucial.

It Takes Time

Just as an acorn grows into a sapling over time, and the oak tree takes decades to mature, dreamers also require long periods of stillness to mature into *curanderas*/healers/artists.

The following dreams are examples of how slowly destiny revealed itself to me. In 1977, about six months into the journals, I had an initiation dream that gave me, so to speak, the assignment to turn "night into day." It took many years before I understood the spiritual nature of this dream. Nevertheless, it brought a new awareness to my attention. Without being conscious of the tasks lying ahead of me, I recognized that my mind, body, and spirit needed integration. The dream left me with the feeling of anticipation, but I could not put my finger on this quiet sense of knowing. I had just graduated from the University of California in Berkeley. I was thirty-four years old and working as an administrator in a patents and trademarks law firm.

First, a short note on kivas will help in understanding the dream. In the Southwestern United States, cultures have kivas, underground holy sites, and that's where this dream takes place.

Initiation

I'm in a kiva, standing on a wooden platform when I become conscious. I look at the light and colors—soft blues, greens, and purples. Dragon-like figures floating toward me, around and away, like fish swimming around seaweed. People gather to participate as witnesses in an initiation. My task is to bring light to darkness.

I recognize a strong, tall, large Indian woman with a tinge of expectancy in her demeanor.

"I'm glad you're here," I tell her.

"I wouldn't have missed this for the world," she replies with a broad smile.

I feel the support of my family as I gaze around the gathering and see they also wait in anticipation.

The scene shifts to a meadow in the forest, but the platform remains constant. I look down and see furry black creatures with long bodies and octopus-like legs meandering about as though they understood the magnitude of this gathering. I have the strange sensation of feeling mildly frightened and confident all at once. An animal that looks like a dog grips its teeth around my ankle. I don't move, and my gaze upon him makes him loosen his hold. He looks up and smiles. "Everyone has her own set of animals to contend with," I hear a woman explaining, but I do not see her. The voice is gentle and calming. I understand her metaphor, and I begin to relax a little. I focus my attention on the sound of her voice as though waiting for further instruction from her.

"Turn night into day," she encourages.

I stand with my feet apart, arms in open position, my head back, and I whisper, "Night into day."

A moment passes and I take a deep breath. I get down on my knees with my arms stretched before me with my forehead to the floor. I repeat, louder this time, "Night into day."

On the third try, a clap of thunder breaks through the clouds, and the sun appears dimly and grows brighter. The animals disappear, and the atmosphere goes from somber to joyous. An orchestra plays background music, and I hear laughter. I breathe a sigh of relief because I have passed the test.

The initiation dream has significance on at least two levels.

First, the voice coming from a person I could not see is from a spirit being giving me specific guidance. The voice may have been Grandmother, or it may have been another guide. I do not recall the specifics of my relationship with the voice. But the voice planted a seed and aroused my curiosity regarding its origin.

Secondly, destiny was wrapped in this dream. I was told to turn "night into day." I was given a task that appeared to be accomplished within the dream— when darkness became day. However, I continued as a child lost in the woods. Occasionally, I would ponder the meaning of the dream. In everyday life, I was a marked woman who neither fit in the business world, nor had anywhere else to turn. I began to look for clues to the meaning of the metaphor.

As I followed my intuition in the months after this dream, I felt a yearning for meaning in life. Changes happened beyond my control, and *a few years later* I received the second directive that defined the task more clearly. Meanwhile, I was learning the lessons of patience—not to push when I had the urge to rush, not to pull when I was anxious to draw something toward me. And, most important, I was learning to receive Spirit's subtle directive by waiting and remaining conscious. I cannot say today that I always do this perfectly, but the intention is there. I am still learning the lessons about knowing when to act spontaneously in my waking life, and when to remain still.

The second directive, which came in the *"El Poder de la Montaña"* dream, showed destiny's persistence and its awesome gifts. It occurred in 1981, five years into the journals, with a gap of four years between this and the "Initiation" dream. Up to that point, I had rambled from job to job, waiting for inspiration to direct me. At the time of this dream, I was conducting a personal retreat, attempting to define my career goals. The dream gave me a mission. I dropped out of the business world without remorse, and immediately began to develop my gifts as a healer. Within three months, I developed a curriculum to teach meditation, slow-movement exercises, and dream awareness classes; and within a year I was enrolled in the counseling program at San Francisco State University.

El Poder de la Montaña
(Power of the Mountain Spirit)

Mamá and I walk through the woods in search of a new home for me. I hear the music of a violin coming from a house where we hear a party going on. I listen. The notes are sweet, soft, and pure. We turn our steps in the direction of the music and come upon a house that is part of a large estate. We walk into the kitchen, and I am taken aback by the tacky plastic 1950s dinette.

"I don't think I like this place," I whisper, but Mamá takes no notice of my reluctance.

"Wait and see," she insists impatiently, and pulls me along in tow.

Assuming I can put what I don't like into storage, I continue to explore through the house and find a bedroom with a canopy bed made up with rich white linens and a soft down quilt. "And this is just one of the smaller rooms," I comment. I've forgotten about the party, and besides, no one seems to be around.

The master bedroom is sunny, with a southern view of the woods, light filtering through the trees. A big, soft bed with similar linens, and private bath face into the woods. The setting is even more luxurious than the first bedroom. My excitement increases when I realize it also has a fireplace.

We walk into a living room where the beauty is simply breathtaking. The plush, soft chairs and sofas are exquisitely arranged around the room facing toward a rock garden. A lush oriental carpet gives it a warm look, making it inviting and comfortable.

When I turn my head, I see this is no mere "rock garden." A large plate glass window opens onto a mountain. I stop dead in my tracks. A solid granite rock as big as El Capitan looms over the house like a specter. I sense a ghastly spirit, disquieting and foreboding. A feeling of strangling suffocation paralyzes me.

Imposed upon by a formidable opponent, I must come to attention. I decide I cannot live here. I am close to doubling over with fear and declaring defeat, when I feel something holding me frozen in my steps. As I observe the sensations rippling through me, I stand firm and begin to breathe into this energy. Gradually the intensity subsides. What initially appears to be a menacing presence is transformed into a tender and embracing feeling. The longer I bask in the spirit of the rock, the stronger and more pronounced this evolving presence becomes.

I sit down on a comfortable chair and face toward the mountain to hold the experience as long as possible. I discover that there is a skylight above me. Apparently, a psychiatrist can meet her clients in this room and look to the stars for direction and guidance.

My awareness of the presence continues to deepen, and I discover that I am participating in a give-and-receive relationship with it. It isn't just any mountain. Its vibrations extend from the epicenter of the rock, a gracious unfolding of radiance and warmth that reverberates in me and enlivens me in its like, passing through and stretching me with it beyond the boundaries of the world and into infinity.

Notable about this dream was the fear that arose upon encountering the spirit of the mountain. The solid granite rock as big as *El Capitán* that loomed over the house like a specter was a spirit distinct from a spirit being in the sense discussed in the previous chapters: succinctly stated, *it is the Great Spirit reflected in nature.*

This dream illustrates that the dreamer must remain steadfast—fear or no fear. During encounters with spirits of this magnitude, we must struggle to remember who and what we are. Ordinarily, one brings the puny little self of the ego and forgets one's true vastness.

As I study the appearance of Spirit over time, I see that it is merciful. At the time, my life didn't seem to suggest any signs of worthiness, nor that I was doing anything in particular to call Spirit or the dream to me. But, I think that my attempts and efforts to reach for it were sincere, and Spirit took compassion upon me. The overwhelming fear I felt was tempered by the spaces between the breaths. By remembering to relax, I overcame the paralyzing fear that gripped me. My saving grace was that I stayed focused and did not cower. I learned that Spirit requires a "pushing back," a tenacity, and attention. This phase of dream awareness must be attained to receive the gift it offers.

Quite unintentionally, I befriended the presence by staying focused and not abandoning the dream for safety. First the mountain dared me to come to attention, and once it had my attention, and I did not draw back from it or cower before it, I became privy to the gift of seeing Spirit's magnificent splendor. When the spirit of the mountain revealed itself to me, I felt my consciousness touch the outer reaches of the universe, and this informed me that I was one with All That Is. The beauty of its power and force is indescribable.

Working with the dream, I next considered becoming a psychiatrist. Previously, I'd had no inclination to go into psychology. Psychology was reserved for white men who had the money necessary to attend years of graduate school. In the dream, I incorporated the skylight as a tool with which I could bring light to the shadows in my life and to others, and the stars somehow planted within me the seed of my becoming a counselor/healer.

Finally, I had to grow a container to house the immensity of the gift so that I could become the healer and integrate what was given. This was a time-sensitive task that occurred with the passing of years. I was privy in this dream to see, under the amplification of the universal telescope, the power that keeps the planets in motion, lights up the billion stars we see at night, lights up our solar system, and enlivens us each with the vital force of life. This was the gift given to me. At first I merely felt the awe of its all-encompassing sacredness. Its full impact came slowly.

Filled with the passion to pass on the message I had received, I tried to tell others about it, but they were too busy trying to figure out their own lives. At one point, I even discussed my dilemma with a spirit being in my dreams, and he merely shrugged his shoulders saying, "I know it."

The important thing was that I did take the dream seriously and began teaching dream awareness, slow-movement exercises, and meditation classes. And, feeling unprepared for the task, I signed up for a graduate program in counseling to help me develop the skills needed to fulfill the calling.

Unfortunately for me, I began to see a professional license as the vehicle for living out my destiny. And when my advisor threatened to report me to the Board of Behavioral Sciences if I did not desist from teaching these classes, I listened and stopped.

A Steady Unfolding

A dream I had late in my story illustrates how destiny's message unfolded in a steady, methodical manner. It occurred thirteen years after the "*El Poder de la Montaña*" dream. I was in a period of deep despair, ill, and unable to go for walks. I had long days to watch the shadows move slowly across the eastern side of my garden.

The dreams of that time showed me that it was my duty to figure out the meaning of this unfortunate turn in my health and fortunes. I had no other choice but to contemplate my *razón de ser*—my reason for being. The urgency to honor something within gnawed more than ever. Despite my intense feelings of unworthiness, destiny persisted in its thrust. All I could do was rise in the morning, write my dreams down, and practice yoga. During this period of significant distress, I had the following dream that set the stage for the next task.

The Assignment

After fifteen years from my first meeting with the elders, I make a visit to the kiva where we first met. They are gathering to select someone for the task of recording the wisdom of oral history.

They debate quietly amongst themselves, some nodding their heads in agreement with each other; others engaged actively in heated discussion. Light reflects on their faces from the fire in the center of the room where they sit on the ground in a semicircle. They want someone who has lived a full life and whose wisdom can be imparted to future generations.

At the start of open discussion, a woman looking like a double of myself walks into the room and a silence falls upon the air. One of the elders looks at me and assents with a slight movement of his head that says, "She is The One"—the obvious choice. The woman's entrance is so exquisitely timed that, for a moment, I doubt the reality of the situation and think that perhaps this has been a staged scenario.

No, this is real, and she is The One, I concur inwardly. She exudes a humility that will play an important part in the transmission of teachings from the Ancient Ones.

How could it be, I mused? After years of trying to decipher my encounters with spirit beings, I wondered whether, in fact, the elders were giving me a directive. The nod of their ascent when my double walked into the kiva was my cue. The impulses in my heart were too dramatic to ignore. At that instant, it occurred to me that the scribbles—my journals—connecting me to other worlds needed to be examined under a magnifying glass and aligned with the outer world.

Going Deeper into My Journals

My husband and I kept an extra layer of curtains over the bedroom windows to keep the room comfortably dark in the mornings. We lived surrounded by pine, bay laurel, and oak trees, and I could hear the rustling of the leaves in the soft, late summer breeze. It was about seven o'clock. Hearing the chirping of birds, I lay in bed for several minutes, staring at the dream catcher hanging from the ceiling. The darkened room felt reassuring. Maybe I was stretching it, I thought as I lay there, but I went to work.

Three years later, I had a four hundred-page manuscript that I submitted to publishers. Fifty or sixty letters later, I still was short of the desired goal. It occurred to me that I needed to look at this in a more formal way. The dreams threaded a tapestry of images together, a narrative that told strange and wonderful stories, yet I had no name for it. Obviously, something needed to be defined more clearly. The task was daunting, and the role my journals told of seemed just as formidable; I saw that embracing the power of the gift was crucial. As a writer, I was stunned with what lay ahead.

For about three years running, every September I investigated colleges and universities where I could work on a doctorate. I would get as far as finding out what the tuition was and stop there. But, finally, there was no denying that the time had come and that the manuscript needed a broader platform on which to stand. As destiny would have it, a friend put me in touch with a woman who became a kindred spirit. Through her, I found a funding source for the research.

The urge to decipher the puzzle and find a connection to the past pushed me like a relentless slave master. As I investigated, I was amazed when I discovered the dream traditions of the early Mesoamerican and Native American Cultures. I came to realize that "The Assignment" was actually a dream revealing my destiny; now I understood why the forces within the dream were driving me to externalize the story. I came to realize that the power of *El Destino*, be it subtle or blatant, is as persistent as a bulldozer preparing the ground for something new to be built.

I found a critical key in the stories of goddesses leaving their communities to gather and/or restore their power. A time comes when a *curandera*/medicine woman must honor her duty as preserver of the culture. She also comes to recognize that her lot will not be an easy one, and that it is not freely given.[73]

How extraordinary it was to be looking at another facet of destiny—an appointment to bring forth that which has been hidden from view up here in *El Norte* for five hundred years!

The early dream of Grandmother inviting herself on this journey; the "Initiation" dream, asking me to bring light into the shadows; "*El Poder de la Montaña*," showing me the foundation of the universe, and the assignment dream giving me the task—these dreams were spread out over twenty-three years. Destiny had revealed itself to me with its relentless, inexorable power. The difficulties of my life—the fragile connection to my name and family, my mother's death when I still needed her, the loss of community and culture—I could understand these now and bear up under them with determination. This was the year 2000, after some interesting twists in the road.

Summary

The inner teachers that guide us through the process of discovering our destinies also will guide us as we dream the next stage of our lives. Destiny, mind, body, and spirit go hand in hand.

Your life and your particular way of developing and manifesting the gifts will reveal themselves to you. In my experience, first came the "Initiation" dream knocking me over the head to get my attention. Then "*El Poder de La Montana*" stretched my consciousness across the universe and revealed my destiny. "The Assignment" dream gave me a task that required research and took several years to complete. That's the wonder of destiny; it enlists our service with or without our consent.

In the past, the Tlamitamines were the learned ones who helped people decipher their destinies. Today, it is our job as healers, at the very least, to trust the universe and take the steps necessary to fulfill our roles. But there is risk in this; not only within the powerful dream, but also in the smaller things: in producing the painting to be displayed in public, the poem or story that needs to be recited at vigils after someone has died or at a baptism, or at the stretching out of hands for healing. There is risk in all of these, and though seemingly small acts, each require courage.

Whatever you do, remember that the fear you feel when facing the frightful camouflages of the spirit equals the intensity of power hidden behind those dreadful masks.

Remember too, that as you use the gifts bestowed upon you, you'll find them accessible and amplified. Destiny brings with it the tools and skills to carry out what it demands of you.

In setting aside our comfortable lives, though we face a future in the unseen and the unknown, the essence of power will grow within, and we will be called toward transformation. In stripping ourselves of notions of safety and comfort, our connection to the old dream traditions as a *curandera*/artist/mystic crystallizes. There's an abundance of metaphors and symbols for those times when isolation is forced upon us and we wander confused and bewildered. These are the times when the heart is stretched, the spirit matures, and we learn a deeper meaning of love, acceptance, and power. These periods of transformation are priceless because they force us into a corner where we have no choice but to surrender to Spirit's calling.

Destiny beckons. For the dreamer who knows the unexplainable, the task is defined for her upon her entry into other worlds, meeting spirit beings, and receiving directives. Her destiny becomes as obvious as the daylight that follows night. When we hear its call, we hasten. And, it brings with it the gifts of power necessary to obey its command.

Most important, in responding to destiny's call, we are taking action on behalf of our culture. We are providing another avenue to meet the community's needs through the songs, poetry, and symbols that we create. Whether acting out of a need for self-expression or for the community's sake, everyone benefits.

CHAPTER 7

▼

Sacred Gifts

A group of students are filming their instructor's lecture in the Financial District where I am having lunch on a low stone wall. The professor, a stocky Mexican man with black wavy hair, announces in his tutorial voice, "You must sing your song. When you have a song, you must sing it out joyously." With his lecture concluded, he breaks into song—beautiful waves of energy flow from his lips like the music of silver bells. A luscious melody resounds in my being, and the world stops to listen reverently. "Just sing your song. Everyone has a song to sing. Belt it out." He laughs sweetly.

The topic *sacred gifts*, most often merely called *power*, is vast and multileveled. As mentioned in the previous chapter, destiny calls and leaves directives and brings with it the tools to follow through. For us as dreamers, taking action is as important as receiving destiny's request. This chapter explores sacred gifts and how they manifest to the dreamer. The dreamer's responsibility is to honor the gifts and follow the dictates of destiny according to the power that the gifts impart to you. Gifts of healing, seeing the future and the past, anticipating death, creative endeavors, and the like—carry with them responsibility to the spirit realm. These gifts are for the perpetuation and empowerment of the community. Their unfolding happens while we participate in listening and doing our part in making our mind, body, and spirit ready for them. Gifts of healing keep alive the traditions of the past and assist in bringing meaning to the community; the symbols that the artist creates are enlivened with Spirit, and this aliveness, as left for us in the traditions of the *Red and Black Ink Books*, also benefits the community.

As we follow the directives, we come to understand "power" and how it operates. Action turns into the awareness of things unseen. Seeing the greatness of power and its effects leaves the dreamer humbled. When you have witnessed this greatness, life is shaped by a sense of responsibility to impart its message to humanity. The gift no longer is only "mine," but is rather a message of love and activism, a gift to be shared with the community and the world, much as the Christian tradition regards gifts of the Spirit.

A gift can be transmitted through a vision or colossal dream and be understood as a divine or cosmic force in the universe. A gift can also be used for the betterment of the world: such gifts define our destiny.

A good example of a gift revealing itself through vision can be seen in Black Elk's life. The Lakota holy man of the nineteenth century was nine when he received his great vision—a dream that lasted several weeks, while he seemed to be unconscious and near death. In his early years, he was guided by the wisdom of an elder medicine man who, soon after Black Elk's visionary event, "saw" that he was destined to walk a sacred path. As Black Elk continued to mature, he took on the role of spiritual guide and healer for the Lakota people.

Sacred gifts manifest in any number of ways that are synonymous with knowledge, maturity, and capability; and the gifts that come forth bring with them the power to accomplish the task that has been assigned. The forces at work within the dreamer are real, formidable, and require strength to withstand. Redefining reality and integrating mind, body, and spirit occurs simultaneously; nevertheless, this long process is quite unnerving.

The acquisition of visions for sacred gifts may occur through ritual preparation and isolation, or may occur spontaneously—especially for women—in dreams or waking time. A vision bestows upon the candidate the power necessary to meet the tasks set forth by destiny, but the power may become noticeable either immediately, gradually, or it may take years to become fully realized.[74] The unraveling of our lives is the background tapestry in which this metamorphosis occurs.

In many of the Creation Stories, the Creatrix goes into isolation to harness her power for the next stage of creation.[75] For the *curandera*/medicine woman, isolation is key to the inward journey. Unfortunately, for those who live away from the culture as I do, outside the Southwest, the communities that support a *curandera's* path are few and far between. Alone, you may not see or understand the spiritual signposts that are calling you to your destiny. There are many ways to go into psychological isolation, a kind of symbolic hibernation that produces the conditions necessary for harnessing power. By putting these experiences that entail a deep inward journey in the context of destiny's beckoning, these periods can bear the fruit required by Spirit.

Three elements can manifest in the course of receiving the vision of empowerment. The first element is the dreamer's expressed fear or anxiety—tangible nearness that impacts the dreamer through the sense of touch, sight, or smell—and a call from the spirit that initially appears threatening, but results in an integrative and positive experience. Being able to withstand fear indicates a maturity or readiness to receive empowerment from the spirit world. The second and third elements are awe and amazement—unmistakable parts of the visionary experience if the dreamer has persisted,[76] an experience such as I encountered in "*El Poder de la Montana*" when I withstood the initial fear of the mountain's spirit. The dreamer's life is then imprinted with a gold seal of authenticity to go forth and impart its message.

In the transfer of power, the spirit of a natural element can reveal itself to the dreamer. You remember Roaming Chief, a Pawnee I spoke of earlier who received power from the spirit of Mother Cedar. In the songs Roaming Chief received, he was empowered by Mother Cedar and given a gift by which to reawaken the awareness of her spirit. The songs Mother Cedar gave him were sung as part of the ceremony of the Pitahawirata Bear Dance, and as the song was sung, the Presence of Mother Cedar recreated the sacredness of the ritual that benefited the community.[77]

In other traditions, power can reveal itself quite differently. For example, even today the Maya see dreaming of a dead relative as a power perceived by the dreamer. That person is initiated into the society of Mayan Daykeepers who practice dream interpretation, cure the ill, and make offerings to the deceased. These gifts do not come easily, because remembering the dream can be a formidable challenge. For these reasons, the Maya believe that the dream itself will struggle against the dreamer to be forgotten, and the dreamer needs power to remember the message that was conveyed to her.[78]

Daykeepers believe that power is also evidenced in the ability to see the future and healing in dreams. Through this calling, they communicate with their deities, are able to diagnose illness, and be apprised of future events. In this tradition, the forces of good, evil, and death are themes of power with which the dreamer struggles.[79]

Within the Aztec tradition, a crucial power is discussed in the *Books of the Red and Black Ink*. Empowerment received could also be transmitted through the dreamer/artist's craft, be it healing or art, music, dance, or other sacred gift. The product of the artist's craft then, emanates or transmits the power that created it to the receiver/observer. The work of the *curandera*/artist/musician/writer is enlivened with power.[80] But, bear in mind that these gifts are not "handed over" easily, and the dreamer must be dedicated to withstand the overwhelming forces that come with it—forces that can be frightening and even terrifying.

The Message

For me, the message of *"El Poder de la Montana"* dream set my life afire to teach dream meditation. Yet, because power has become diffused in our culture, it felt as though I were pregnant and had no *partera*—midwife—to help me through it.

With threats from counselors, teachers, and state agencies, I discontinued the pursuit of my mission in life as I saw it then. They thought the classes I had developed in slow-movement, meditation, and dream awareness—which had been the cause of my returning to school—were in conflict with the training. My mistake lay in my having tried to make a spiritual process into something linear. To me, it looked normal and natural to pursue a master's degree and subsequent state licensing; where I fell off track was in thinking that I needed permission to heed Spirit's call.

Regardless of how I interpreted the meaning of my dreams, the power I witnessed emanating from *"El Poder de la Montana"* dream became the guiding torch that illumined my commitment. I was determined to teach what I had seen, and I resolved to continue my work with The Center for Attitudinal Healing in a different format. In some crucial manner, I had let myself be distracted because, in truth, the gift was overpowering, and I felt ill prepared to handle it.

Death Shows Compassion

I became aware of a type of gift that struck a familiar chord for me in the Omaha Owl Dreamers and their society called *Wanaoxe ithaethe*—"those to whom the ghost has shown compassion."[81] To these visionaries were given the power to see imminent death.

I began to see death in dreams very early in the journals. First, I would have the dream that announced someone's death or developing illness, and as events occurred in the waking state, I would understand the meaning of the dream. Sometimes, however, the prophecy in a dream would take many years to come to pass, such as in 1976, when I dreamed a childhood friend's husband had cancer. He died suddenly four years later after a short battle with cancer. I also dreamed that my father was in a wheelchair. He was seventy-six at the time and still quite healthy. Ten years passed before I saw him in a wheelchair.

The doors for the gifts opened for me when I began to work with families at The Center. There, as a part of my internship at San Francisco State University, I facilitated the support person's group for people who had loved ones with life-threatening illnesses. I also began working with the persons who had the life-threatening illnesses. As my relationships with them developed, I noticed a certain rhythm when they neared death, and I saw in advance the unfolding of the person's destiny.

For example, I had three dreams and events blended together in two successive nights in 1984 that alerted me to a friend's impending transition. These dreams happened about two years after *"El Poder de La Montaña"* dream. Kendra (not her real name) and I were meeting informally, and that included my visits to her in the hospital. On several occasions, she had recovered from near-death encounters, appeared to be doing well, and then suddenly was readmitted. But her tenacious hold on life was weakening, and she persisted until exhaustion overtook her. I visited her at the hospital the day of the first dream.

Draped Mirrors

Kendra, looking very strong and vibrant, and her husband, Jason take me to their home, and we enter through the back door into a utility room that leads to a larger room that serves as a family/dining room.

Along the walls of the room are several mirrors. Jason leaves to do something upstairs, and Kendra walks toward one of the mirrors and pulls on a chord as though adjusting a Venetian blind to let in more light. Instead, black drapes roll down the mirrors.

Then, she walks toward the air conditioner, presses the "on" button, and leaves the room. I hear the conditioner starting up, and cold drafts of air begin to circulate around the room. I rub my arms vigorously to keep myself warm, but the chill goes all the way to the bone.

The black cloths draping over the mirrors were my first clue that death was imminent. In her culture, when someone dies, draped mirrors are required for the period of bereavement. That death was imminent was further confirmed to me through the bone-chilling air. In the air's chill, I sensed how her absence would impact her family with a feeling of irreversible longing.

The dream that follows is the second of three that occurred. After not visiting for several days, I stopped by the hospital one Tuesday afternoon. That night, after facilitating the support group at The Center, I retired for bed at eleven o'clock.

Compassion Awaits

It must be around 11:30 or 12:00 midnight, because I have just drifted off to sleep when I find myself floating through the hospital corridor. The lights are glaringly white, and I shade my eyes from them. I turn into K's room.

"When do you think you'll be leaving?" I ask.

Not saying anything, she indicates that she has some trepidation about it.

Like a flashback, I see that her ancestors are waiting for her on the other side, and I utter some assurance.

'You've suffered enough,' I tell her before leaving.

This was a straightforward experience in which *I actually visited her hospital room and had that conversation.* I felt disoriented under the bright lights, which gives me reason to believe that I actually was there.

Then I had a third dream that was so graphically visceral that I have no doubt that I escorted her to the next realm.

Transition

It's three o'clock in the morning, and I begin having sensations of suffocation and great difficulty breathing. There is a total absence of light, more profound than anything I've ever experienced. I choke and gasp for air, stretch my neck and arch my back to let my lungs expand. I begin falling down a chute, falling, falling, and not knowing where I am going. In this utter chaos, I notice K. is following me.

Finally, we hit bottom, a tiny island of moist soil near the edge of a flowing river. I see a group of people, and the first person I recognize is my mother standing on dry ground smiling happily. She and several of K's family are waiting for her. There is music in celebration of her arrival. I want to hug my mother, but she holds up her hand, telling me I shouldn't cross the river. I realize I am escorting K. from her life on Earth to her next life, and now it is time for us to say goodbye. She is ready to stay, and steps across the narrow stream of water that separates us from the group.

Moments later, lying flat on my back, I opened my eyes to check my waking senses. I was struck with the certainty that Kendra had passed on and that I had guided her to the other side. In the terrifying choking sensations, I actually experienced a sympathetic death with her. Despite the nightmarish quality of the experience, I remained focused and discovered that my friend was accompanying me. Between the choking and seeing my mother, I realized that I had escorted her to the "other side." Seeing Kendra step across the narrow stream, I observed that she had accepted her readiness to move on to her next life.

When morning came, my feelings that I had traveled to the boundary of a new frontier were further confirmed. At a quarter of eight, I was sitting at my desk looking for Kendra's home telephone number, when her husband called to let me know she had passed on at two thirty that morning. He also relayed a dream he'd had wherein he had seen her waltzing with her grandfather.

"Yes, she's doing just fine," I assured him.

Another experience I had with death announcing itself concerned a friend who had been full of life and had no traces of disease. The premonition came about nine months in advance of the events that played out.

Ellen

I sit at the edge of the bed clutching the drenched white handkerchief. I am sobbing uncontrollably because my friend Ellen is going away, and I will not see her again for a long, long, time.

When I encountered friends or family in dreams, I normally checked out the content of the dream with them. So, upon waking from this dream, I called Ellen to see what was happening in her life, whether she was, in fact, leaving the area.

"Are you thinking of leaving us?" I asked casually after talking about the dream.

She said something in a tone of voice that discouraged further discussion, so I put the thought aside. But a few months later as we had dinner one warm August evening under the umbrella of an old sprawling oak tree, she brought it up again.

"Remember that dream you had of me?'

"Yeah, of course," I answered.

"It sort of scares me. Several of my family have died at forty-five, and I'll be there in November."

I didn't know what to say. I couldn't honestly say, "Well, I wouldn't worry about it. It probably doesn't mean anything," because something had rung true about the dream, and I knew she was terrified. I stopped chewing on the salad and waited for further comment from her. Ellen and I were accustomed to talking about death because we had lost many friends in connection to our work at The Center.

I have a picture of Ellen sassily smoking a cigarette on a spacious deck surrounded by trees at The Center's Christmas party that winter. The months passed, and on Easter Sunday of the following year, while shopping with a friend, without warning, she had a cardiac arrest and never regained consciousness. She passed on three weeks later. I missed her terribly, just as I had in the dream. With loss accumulating in my heart, I sobbed uncontrollably and was nearly suicidal.

Seeing through My Hands

Another example of knowing that death was near came through my hands as I worked with life-threatening illness. I began to sense death as I ran my hands along someone's aura, a startling feeling of emptiness. Other times it might be an impression of hollowness in their eyes, as though the soul had already begun its journey home.

In 1976 I had a dream of my father in a wheelchair, and I put the thought in the back of my mind. When I heard his health was failing him in 1986, it did not come as a great surprise to me. It felt as though I were entering a surreal world in which I knew what lay ahead.

Ten years after anticipating my father's demise, I received news that he had been hospitalized and that he would soon be making his transition.

Adios Padre

> *I remember walking down the hallway toward his hospital room, and seeing his little body. My father, the giant of my life, is in the fetal position. I run my hand over his aura, and feel a flatness that indicates an absence of his aura. Nothing. That means there is little time left. Two weeks, maybe, I conclude. That's all I remember of the visit. I don't remember if he opened his eyes; whether he recognized me; or, even, whether we spoke.*

When I looked back on the sequence of events of that afternoon and the time of his death, I realized that I had slipped into denial. In a strange way, I went into some kind of amnesia, and followed through on my wedding plans. He died three days after the wedding within the two-week period that I had foreseen.

Protection around the Heart

The topic of death and seeing the future emphasizes another issue, which is that you may be given information that is difficult to accept. As a dreamer, you will be given the strength to face the facts of life as they develop, especially when they concern a loved one. I think that there is a protection around the heart, because when I saw my father's approaching death, I took a wait-and-see attitude without feeling the pain of impending loss.

Each dreamer is unique in her experience. We know that no two witnesses at one event will report the same version of the story. In the same way, dream life is particular to a dreamer, and the constellation of dream events will vary for everyone. The point here is to take the information seriously and recognize this is an area of dreaming that has an ancient and sacred tradition.

Power, Patience, and Sacred Gifts

Before I went back for my doctoral studies, I had heard of power, but believed that it was something medicine people had or used to accomplish feats of great wonder and awe. As I studied the types of power and sacred gifts discussed in the sources, I concurred with Irwin that in many instances, power is revealed in the quiet manifestation of a life accomplishing ordinary tasks.[82]

A gift is for the community, for its perpetuation and its spiritual growth. Be willing to risk what you fear most about bringing forth the gift. Giving is the blessing. There is no other promise of something to come, only your personal recognition that a miracle has occurred, and that you have complied with the will of the Creatrix.

A dream that spoke to me of the essence of patience and endurance came when I was in my late forties. I had been keeping a journal for nearly fifteen years and thought I was a mature woman; yet the dream advised me to mature further by blending with the terrain of the dreamscape; it told me to persevere and wait.

El Secreto de Mi Mamá
(My Mother's Secret)

I haven't seen my mother for years when she appears to me one morning looking like I remember her—not with the matted hair and gnarled gray fingernails, nor as the raving madwoman I saw in the early years after her death—but like herself. She wears a white camisole loosely tied at the collar with a pink satin ribbon, and her hair is casually rolled back from her face. She looks happy and peaceful, and her skin has a freshly powdered look. Sitting under the blankets at the head of the bed with her legs crossed, and I, sitting on the opposite side facing her, we begin to converse telepathically. I want to hug her, but she motions with a wave of her hand to stay put. "I'm here for a reason," she informs me. In dreamtime years, I am twenty-five and my hair must be long because I notice that the three hairpins on my lap will not be sufficient to hold it up.

"When you are older," she continues.

I hear her, but the importance slips by. I keep studying the hairpins, wondering how I can comb my hair. I think about my spiritual search, and that I haven't shared it with her or even mentioned my dream journals.

"When you are older," she repeats.

This time her words reach me. I suddenly realize she and my Tía Elena have planned from my early childhood my participation in a society of women who pass on sacred teachings. She, my aunt, and grandmother had been members of this society of curanderas *all their lives, and no one knew of this, not even their husbands. In fact, even I am not privy to the actual operations of this group. The sad part is that I will have to wait many more years to have them revealed.*

As though begging for candy, I doggedly tug at her to say more, but she remains steadfast.

"That's all you need for now," she says.

What was that "secret society" my mother and aunt had planned for me, I wondered. In my youth, I had heard nocturnal conversations between my mother, my aunt, and grandmother in my grandmother's cottage in Salamanca, Guanajuato. I would fall asleep to their stories of times long since passed, during the Mexican Revolution of 1910, and the turbulence they had lived through. I didn't know it at the time, but I was being infused with their images of *aquellos tiempos*—those times—a Mexico that contained *comadres, compadres*, family traditions, deceased family members, candlelit altars, busy kitchens, and magical stories that lived in their bones. I was being handed those torches of the heart for which no words exist. And along with those memories, I was receiving other guidance meant only for me—about my lineage, my particular history—intended for my grounding in life. In this dream, "My Mother's Secret," the gift of power is implied: in her words, "When you are older," the seed that had been planted in those years when I visited my grandmother was still germinating. Nonetheless, I needed to wait.

Even Black Elk faced the uncertainty of his relationship with the Grandfathers who had bestowed upon him the gifts he had received as a boy. During that time when the traditions of his culture remained intact, his life was purposeful and intense. When the Lakota culture was devastated by the European invasion, his life changed dramatically. Doubts overshadowed him, and he finally left his community for a sideshow existence with Buffalo Bill. For two years, he wandered afar in Europe, bereft in mind, body, and spirit. Even as a mature man, he know-ingly submitted to the teachings of missionaries innocently attempting to illumi-nate his mind.

Much later, as an aging man, he stood on Harney Peak and called upon the Six Grandfathers, unsure whether they would respond to his call. With the pass-ing of decades, even with years of healing the sick and the unfolding of prophe-cies, he doubted the greatness bestowed upon him. What he had seen in his vision was vast, beyond the comprehension of a humble human being, and he felt he had fallen far short of that vision.[83]

Power demands patience, and that patience rises out of profound trust in the forces that shape our lives, and for those we are to serve. Living up to its demands will leave you limp and exhausted, and you, my dear *comadre*, my sweet sister, will wonder at your worthiness of the gift. This dream map intends to help you bypass any shadow of doubt that may arise.

Summary

The types of power we receive reflect the tasks necessary to carrying out our des-tiny, a delicate process always unfolding. Poetry, music, dance, story are for shar-ing. We share them at *bautismos, bodas, velorios*—baptisms, weddings, wakes—and fiestas. The symbols and images that we receive are for splashing in gigantic proportions on public buildings, creating murals with brilliant and radiant colors. Art has a life and contains the vibrancy of nature. Your part as receiver of the gift is to bring it forth and tell the story. Spirit takes care of the rest.

How we use what we've been given becomes more of an issue with the passage of time. Urgency pushes through our fingers, and our music becomes more melodic, sweet, and soothing; our art makes its statement and impacts the beholder with its power; our movement as dancer becomes more expressive. The power of healing that comes through our words or touch reaches its height beyond denial. Externalizing the power for the benefit of humankind becomes essential.

Most important, you the dreamer/*curandera*, must remember that the intention of dreaming is not to attain powers to perform great feats and miracles, but to live your life as close to the dictates of Spirit as possible. Keep moving in the direction that Spirit calls. Spirit will impact you with specific intention and purpose; and the greater forces of the universe will make decisions beyond your control. Your job is to take huge leaps of faith, use the gifts given, and let go of the results. Be willing to be a fool for Spirit. Belt your song out joyously!

C H A P T E R   8

▼

Nature's Aliveness

Dreams overlap categories. The following is actually a portion of a dream that I discuss in greater detail in chapter ten; I include this segment here because it is a good example of how the Divine reveals itself through nature.

I Am the Sun
(A dream segment)

I read the cover letter, a long poem that sends me into a reverie with feelings of wide expanses and power, as though I am hovering above the world with the sun as my torch and guiding light, with freedom to travel to other universes; graceful feelings of joy washing through me.

It occurred to me two years after this dream that in the sensations of power and joy, I had actually experienced emanations from the Sun. As I studied the dream and came back to it many times, the sensations of exquisite joy within it finally brought the message home loud and clear: I *am* the Sun! I am of it. It is of me.

Today, we do not think of the Sun as capable of giving us spiritual power, nor do we see ourselves as being connected to it, other than that it gives us life, light, and warmth. Actually, the aliveness in nature is an invitation to humans to share in its glory. Our ancestors took their expansion of consciousness experiences as evidence of our Creator's vastness and of their own greatness.

Divine Elements of Nature

In earlier chapters, we discussed the Old Dreamers' worldview, and how they understood that the Divine manifested itself in nature. They worshipped all of the elements of nature and gave them names. With this reverence, they remembered to tread lightly upon the earth and to surrender to the greatness within all living things. They also regarded time and space as imbued with the essence of the Divine, and the Four Directions as aiding them in becoming one with it.

Through opposite pairings in nature, the Old Dreamers formulated their practices to help them transcend the mundane and come in touch with the Divine. In the southern point of the Four Quadrants stood *Chalchihuitlicue*, goddess of rain and the consort of *Tlaloc*, God of Rain. Together they caused fertilization, and their abundance caused the seed to sprout. Through them humans had grain to harvest. To the north, their opposite position, stood the Lord of Death and his consort. Each pairing had its role to play as a unit, and each was opposite to the other.[84]

Let's now explore your place in the universe just as the Old Dreamers explored their place in theirs, and appreciate the essence of harmony and unity in all of nature. With the gifts of time and space, awareness, and destiny tucked safely in your medicine bundle, the psychic references we've mentioned will keep them in perspective.

As with gifts of power, Identification with nature requires humility. Today you can acknowledge nature's greatness, and recognize the roots that make us kin to it and allied with it. In relationship with nature, we discover our uniqueness and access true power. As kin to nature, we take our rightful places as daughters of The Mother, made in her likeness. Remember that the universe is an alive and vibrating force: a rock is no longer merely a rock, but rather an element imprinted with Spirit, able to communicate, and as worthy of respect as any other spirit being. You will find in your dreams the reasons the early dreamers saw nature as sacred. Seeing nature's core opens yet another door toward recognizing your purpose and your own divinity.

The Pairing of Opposites

Very early in the journals, I began to see aspects of nature in a most peculiar form. I would see water through a lens that magnified its relationship to the Divine, and this seeing was accompanied with sensations of exquisite joy and beauty. The plight of animals in my dreams alerted me to a possible danger, particularly danger to the bear, but most certainly it led me to question what I normally saw as the bear's role in relation to humans.

Each taken individually, the images were as odd as the early shadows I came upon in my dreams—the shadows that terrified me—but there was something that made me ponder on my definition of reality. The questions that arose took me to a splendor that could not be put into words, but was, nevertheless, imprinted upon my consciousness. These images brought my attention to *the pairing of opposites* that slowly began to change my perception. The polarity I saw in the pairing of opposites explained the forces that shape our lives, and it indicates the importance of deciphering our destiny. Added to that realization, I found the aliveness of nature that reveals itself as we enter other dimensions. The power of the tree from chapter three illustrates the complexity of the many ways nature's aliveness can be observed and experienced.

Here are some examples of how nature revealed itself to me in the pairing of opposites. The following group of dreams occurred in the early 1980s. It was spring, and I had just returned from a weekend in Yosemite Valley where I had seen the two thousand, three hundred-foot waterfall, full and vibrant with ice-cold water, cascading off the magnificent rocks. I was awed by the greatness of the valley and the magnitude of the rocks, but in my dreams, I saw the beauty and spirit my physical eyes had overlooked.

Blessing

The early morning air is cool and crisp against my face as I gaze toward the majestic mountains that encase Yosemite Valley. In the distance, I see sprays of water that the wind is throwing high over the mountaintops. Sometimes the water forms clouds over people and blesses them with ice-cold showers. A man mentions that water travels underground to the top of the mountain.

I decide to make the climb to the top where the river ends and the falls drop. At the top, a long line of people wait to see the waterfall right where it drops to its most prominent power spot. When it is my turn, a terror of stepping to the edge of the precipice grips me. I scurry away from the edge to catch my breath. Aware that I may be passing up a-once-in-a-lifetime opportunity, I decide to come back another time to see the wonder and splendor.

This encounter with the sacred was filled with a sense of expansive well-being; I felt the early morning air indescribably crisp. The sacredness of water was emphasized by the huge sprays shooting over the mountaintops, and by the thunder of the water's crash against the rocks twenty-three hundred feet below, at its prominent "power spot." This encounter in my dreams imprinted on my "seeing," because in my waking life, I had scurried away just as in the dream and had refused to step to the edge of the falls to see its full force. So now I felt the falls were speaking to me directly. "See?" it seemed to say. "This is what you missed." Yes, I had missed my opportunity to see the vital force of water crashing on the rocks; but worse yet, had missed it again when given the opportunity to see it with my spiritual eyes. This dream caught my attention, however, and gave me a new way of seeing the world.

A second dream followed the next night, as though the great height and power that had terrified me was showing me the actual source of my fear—possible union with the Divine!

Yosemite Falls

Holding a photograph of a bride and groom, I look past the bride's veil and notice Bridalveil Falls in the background, awesome and full. Its compelling beauty and power draw me into the photo, and I become Spirit with the fall.

Becoming "Spirit with the fall" gave me a sharp visceral experience that unmistakably confirmed an encounter with the Divine. I was puzzled by the fact that I had felt disconcerted while visiting Yosemite Valley, but these dreams brought me into a relationship in which I saw nature in a new light. It became obvious to me that seeing through Spirit's eyes was the only way to perceive reality.

The following dream, "Water/Fire," came a year after the first two water dreams, and with its coming, I began to wonder whether these dreams were calling my attention to a *personal* kind of power. In my waking life, I was in the throes of relaxing my shoulders with the Autogenic Training in my biofeedback class at San Francisco State University.

Water/Fire

I travel over hill and dale to reach the little house in the mountains. Expecting to find my mother, I encounter an empty house with only a circle of chairs in the living room and a table off to the side. I sit down to wait while the other women arrive.

I look toward the table and see resting on it, a crude obsidian knife with jagged edges. It arouses my curiosity. Sensing it has secret powers, I get up from my chair and draw closer to it.

One of the women comes into the room just as I start eyeing the knife and says, "Don't try to pick it up, because it has a power that will hurt you." Her words only propel me toward the knife.

I pick up the knife, and I am shocked with a tremendous electrical surge that bolts through me. I begin to fly out of control around the room in sharp geometric patterns.

My mother walks in and tells me to come join the circle, in a voice that says, "Quit showing off, and come sit down!" I slow down, return the knife to the table, and go back to my seat. Just then, a boy about eleven years old bursts through the door shouting excitedly, "Mamá, Noni, come and see what's happening." Abandoning the circle, the women run outside.

Beautiful steam/moulten lava and sparks of fire spout out of a volcano. Its beauty leaves us quiet and breathless. I begin to feel a familiar sensation—I am pure spirit, sweet nectar, able to perceive life's details in rhythm to a wondrous song.

When I've had a dream like this, I lie in bed trying to digest the immensity of its meaning. This particular morning, I thought of the passage in the Bible where Moses isn't permitted to look directly into the face of God. So, too, I felt the group had not been permitted a close view of her, as water or fire.

These images of the Divine through liquid fire made lasting impressions that illustrated the interconnectedness of Spirit and the aliveness of nature. I could not help but begin to change my view of the world, of God, and of the purpose for dreaming.

Nagualism/Transmutation

Discussion of the interrelatedness of nature and the Divine get complicated because nagualismo rears its head and confuses the issues. Nagualismo is a concept of transmutation documented in the *Books of the Red and Black Ink* that describes a being changing itself into another form. When we see pairings of opposites, they indicate information on the God of Duality. The stories about the God of Duality also carry the codes for transmutation.

Let's explore how the Creation Stories depict the concept of the Divine impersonating an animal. This concept is important to understanding both the worldview of the Old Dreamers and our present-day awareness of nature's divinity. Oral lore tells us that some dreamers may still have the knowledge necessary for them to transmute,[85] but they are very rare, and the majority of people do not.

Though for most of us, simply remembering the depths of communion with nature certainly is a vital element of being human and carrying out our Destiny.

The opening stanzas of the First Creation Stories make it clear that the transcribers believed that the God of Duality was impersonating an animal.

> The explanation of the mysteries and the illumination
> By Former and Shaper;
> Bearer and Engenderer are their names,
> Hunter Possum and Hunter Coyote,
> Great White Pig and Coati.[86]

One interpretation of these opening lines is that Great White Pig and Coati are "magically impersonating the divine creating forces of the Former and Shaper." Given the relationship between the God of Duality, humans, nature, and time and space, a unified universe is revealed. In their world, everything comes from the substance of our Creator. These few lines indicate that the Divine is present in every aspect of creation. There is no hierarchy, for no aspect of creation is devoid of its presence. Neither human, nor element, nor animal is better than any other.[87] At the same time, the Old Dreamers cultivated the various practices to transmute themselves into other forms.

In my journals, nagualismo also appeared in a way that led me to understand the concept of duality and belief in the possibility of nagualismo. Today, the force of energy that was utilized for transmutation of the body into another species is used for spiritual transformation and freeing oneself of the suffering of the world.

As a culture, we have lost the stories of oral lore that connect us to the aliveness of nature. We are one with nature, and yet our consciousness has strayed so far from the old paradigm that many of us have forgotten about this unity.

The Bear

Many Native American stories are saturated with images of the bear and the power that she offers. The Pawnee Bear Society, imitating movements of the bear in order to receive power from the Sun, performs ceremonies and dance. The bear has tremendous hunting and curative powers. If a medicine person wishes to obtain favor from the bear, or to have the bear as a healing ally, stories and traditions abound that will tell us what we must do to gain good standing with her.[88]

If we wish to be blessed by her grace, we must court her through sacred ceremonies.

Through such images as the bear, we can see how communion occurs and how power is attained. Our inward selves are the fertile soil that receives seed and in those dark, moist places of the spirit, the seed sprouts and grows. The harvest feeds our lives and the lives of others in important ways that we cannot anticipate.

The following dream occurred in such a fertile environment in 1982. It expanded my understanding of the aliveness of nature in general, but it also pointed out how far I had strayed from the bear's consciousness and knowing.

The Bear

> *Wearing a bright yellow shirt, and carrying a large piece of chocolate cake and a pineapple on a silver platter, a young, beautiful Indian maiden gets on the bus I am riding. She sits next to me and flashes a broad, electrifying smile. Her radiance reverberates in my being like tiny butterfly kisses of great joy throughout. We are traveling on a high, narrow levee where water runs quite some distance below us.*
>
> *We pass a concrete apartment complex halfway down the road, and a bear and her cub are scavenging through garbage cans.*
>
> *"They've lost their sense of direction because the environment has changed so much," shouts another passenger from the back of the bus.*

The voice at the back of the bus in "The Bear" dream tells us why we have forgotten about the sacredness of nature—the environment has changed. The mother bear and her cub's scavenging through garbage cans illustrates how far contemporary consciousness has strayed from the sacred. This dream made me aware that the bear's spirit, sacredness, and her plight, have become invisible to us as a culture. We are not respecting other aspects of the Divine by destroying the natural environment of the bear. Eventually, the spirit of the bear was made real to me in a way that enabled me to understand why our Native American ancestors revered it. The consciousness she represents makes available the spiritual connection we have lost in a world of materialism and scientific influence.

But I must not leave out the beautiful smile that electrified my spirit within the dream. The presence of this beautiful woman and her dazzling smile alerted me to the fact that there was something special in the offing.

Other Images from Nature

The following dream, "The Dog," is another example of how the aliveness of nature and Spirit are intertwined.

The Dog

My friend Danielle has a black German shepherd that looks like a wolf. We're in her office, and he is sitting near her old gray metal desk. He has colorful feathers tied to his collar. Looking at me, he raises an eyebrow as though to say something, but I ignore him and continue talking to a friend that has just stopped by the office for a visit.

"Have you noticed the feathers?" Danielle asks me.

I'm not sure why this is important, but I pause for a moment to make a closer inspection. They radiate a beauty that leaves me breathless, as though I were looking upon the dazzle of a million diamond lights.

"Be sure to take note of the feathers," she advises once more. The dog is gentle and loving, and I get the distinct impression I am witnessing a Buddha appearing in the body of a dog.

The dazzling beauty of the feathers is noteworthy. Radiance by itself heralds the message of the sacred.

In each instance, Spirit shows us how to incorporate the new consciousness into our practice toward transformation. But the dream is not just about a personal power or consciousness; it's a message that can call us to attention or awaken our spirit.

Another dream that showed me the sacredness of nature was the "*Caballito*" dream. The joy that I experienced upon my encounter with the spirit of the horse was sheer ecstasy. I had this dream in 1994, when I was in the midst of a medical crisis and was deeply questioning my Christian roots.

El Caballito
(The Little Pony)

My father is flying a single-engine Cessna. My mother, and I are sitting single file behind him. A full silvery moon lights the night sky, and we have clear visibility for miles that stretch over the farmland surrounding us. The air is calm and still as we prepare for takeoff down a narrow strip.

Just as we are gaining speed to lift off, a little pinto breaks away from a herd of horses grazing near the runway and heads toward the aircraft.

"Get going. It's coming after the plane," I shout out in English. "Hurry! Hurry!" I keep shouting anxiously.

The door is open and the pony manages to jump in. He barely makes it by hanging on with his teeth to get on before the plane lifts off. He heads straight toward me. I am terrified that he's going to bite me, not knowing why he is pursuing us. Apparently, he knows me, and with a gentle humor, starts nuzzling my neck playfully. His nose tickles against my cheek, and I start laughing and nuzzling him back, rubbing my face against his jaw and the top of his head.

Again, before the plane gets too far off the ground, he jumps out. I see him stumble, and fear he has broken a leg. Thankfully, he gets up immediately and takes one more look at me before prancing away. I wonder how he knew me, and why he risked his life for me. My heart melts with love for him.

It took me some time to figure out what this pony represented for me, and in the meantime I just tucked the feelings of love and compassion into my pocket, and carried the spirit of the pony around with me, like a little gemstone. On the one hand, it was not only the horse's essence I was seeing. I realized it also represented Jesus Christ's love.

Over the years, these dreams whose animal images brought heightened awareness and exquisite joy provoked much wondering within as I tried to figure out their meaning. I heard the lion's roar, saw the magnificence of the serpent, the wonder and power of the jaguar, and many other creatures. They were real to me, but I didn't understand their connection to the past. Here, they are neatly lined up to call your attention to this consciousness.

It is no wonder that the early religions revered nature, and believed that the Shaper and Former would impersonate creatures, and be embodied in all aspects of creation.

Surfing through our dream journals, we must always remember that the Divine may appear in disguised form. These appearances are a call to awaken or to align our spiritual path with new and more personal meaning. The greatness that you see and feel is yours to use; hold it delicately in your hands, and let its purpose be revealed to you for the benefit of all. As your life unfolds with wondrous gifts of beauty and grace, remember their source.

The following dream—"Forgotten Baskets"—brought all of these dreams together, showing how the universe lives in us and why nature is alive with spirit.

Forgotten Baskets

Driving down a busy thoroughfare in a hilly city like San Francisco, I come upon several beautiful, highly crafted baskets a woman has left on the side of a busy street. The baskets are large enough to serve as luggage, but their weave is also tight enough that they could be used as caldrons for cooking or for boiling water when birthing babies. I wonder who could possibly leave such precious jewels carelessly abandoned and at risk, but I figure she will eventually come back for them. I admire the intricate design of yellow grass, and fine strips of brown leather woven into a Navajo design, and still can't imagine why such beauty has been carelessly discarded, Slowing the car down to a crawl, I drive over them. I am glad to see in the rearview mirror that they have remained undisturbed. Traffic is backing up for several blocks; I feel the hopelessness of the baskets ever surviving the onslaught of traffic.

I come back the same way a couple of days later, only to find that the woman has not yet reclaimed her belongings; but now the baskets are scattered and traffic is at a complete standstill. A heavy sadness overwhelms me, seeing these precious items still unclaimed. My breath becomes irregular as though I am suffocating, and I awaken with my heart palpitating.

I lay in bed quietly studying my dream catcher hanging from the ceiling. The baskets made me think of my medicine bag, which contained my books and sacred objects. The baskets left to block traffic, precious containers and symbols of something sacred, turned my mind to wonder—What have I done?

For about a year after this dream, I looked for an explanation, for the deeper meaning of baskets, and I finally found that baskets contain the psychic power of the weaver.[89] It took me several more years to fully grasp the meaning of the "psychic power of the weaver."

It occurred to me one clear winter night while I was gazing at the stars, that we live in a basket of psychic energy! Then another profound thought occurred to me: we *are* psychic energy—whatever the universe's composition—that's what we are! I saw that the real Weaver of the Basket—the universe—is the Greatest Dreamer of All: Our Creator, the Great Mystery, Corn Woman, the God of Duality, the Tao, Quan Yin, Tara, Kali, Allah, God; all the names humanity has given this mysterious force. How could we as a race not be enlivened with the same wonder? And, how can we exclude nature from it?

Summary

The Mesoamericans and other cultures of the Americas perceived the sacredness of nature as being a part of the whole of creation, wherein it was believed that the Divine impersonated its own creation, be it human or other. In the forces of opposites, the power of creation revealed itself symbolized in a multitude of forms that demonstrated great beauty and power. We have lost our sense of wonder and do not see the magic of creation in nature. But the bear's consciousness is making its way back to us, and the Sun's emanations can fill us with power that will inspire our lives. As we recognize the wisdom of the dog, horse, and all other animal life, we cannot help but be amazed at the Mother's great creation.

When the sacredness of water and the wonder of the Creator as our ancestors perceived it is revealed to us, let's give thanks for the gifts of "seeing" and "knowing." These powers are yours to use in living out your destiny. We become unified with all else that exists, and our separateness gradually dissolves. There is no "other"—not among human beings or in any other aspect of creation. We are one in this great basket of psychic energy. Nature's aliveness shows us that the Creator leaves nothing beyond the reaches of its love and compassion.

CHAPTER 9

▼

Duality

As initiates preparing for their role in the society of old cultures of Mesoamerica worked out the conflicts of duality, they came to another stage that they called "getting a face and heart." Traditionally, The Old Dreamers called this period of darkness "duality." Transcendence and transformation was the reward of the seeker, reserved for the dreamer who was prepared to go to any extremes to unite with truth. Transcendence was attained through arduous labor, strenuous discipline, and dedication.[90]

The *Tlamitamines* used their psychological and spiritual tools to provide initiates with guidance and direction in their paths toward transcending duality. In the initiates' journeys, they underwent challenges that helped them recognize the dissonances within their characters. From the *Tlamitamines'* teachings that included philosophical and historical lectures, the initiates developed character that deepened their existence and gave them strength and understanding to attain their goals.[91]

Today, within our culture, there is no tradition for transcending duality. Primarily, the dreamer/artist is left to her own resources. However, the unraveling of life that begins with the inward journey when she starts tracking her dreams is a necessary and vital aspect of her path toward transcendence. In Western terms, this next stage would be likened to St. John of the Cross's "dark night of the soul." Working her way through duality, she will travel full circle to Corn Woman, the vital force toward transformation.

Psychological Homelessness

For purposes of this chapter in discussing duality and transcendence, I will explore a type of struggle one must encounter: prying loose one's personal demons and healing issues that psychologists term, "psychological homelessness."

Psychological homelessness within the Latina culture is rooted in the historical legacy of oppression, colonization, and a stratified caste system based on race, ethnicity, religion, gender, and ability.[92] When two cultures rub against each other, the cultural and religious values of the oppressed group are invalidated; and the psychic spaces become suffocating and difficult to maneuver through. One writer called these places the "borderlands."[93]

Whatever hardships you have endured in your life—discrimination, alienation, isolation, rejection by a lover or personal abandonment by a parent or child; the challenges of your particular family background; addictions to substances, or behaviors that compromise your standing in the community. Whatever issues may be impeding your movement toward your destiny—you've hit upon psychological homelessness and duality. Take these painful memories and jagged pieces of photographs etched in your heart—and burst through them. This is a time for fearlessness.

The effects of psychological homelessness upon the *curandera*, as painful as they may be, are potential avenues for empowerment and spiritual development. In the final analysis, they form a doorway into the descent that will liberate you. This applies to mystics from all walks of life, especially in a Western scientific culture that denies both the dreamer/mystic's spiritual worldview and the authenticity of her experience.

My Own Experience of Psychological Homelessness

In my story, psychological homelessness continued to plague me into my forties, the early 1990's. I felt alone in the world. No matter how hard I tried to fill the void left by the years of constant change, the emptiness within was unfathomable.

Love eluded me, my health failed me, and many other problems pursued me. I gave into it by trying to build my life around a fundamentalist community. I entered into it tentatively, fearful that I would again find the undesirable benchmarks that I had long ago left behind. But, in spite of these fears, and encouraged by the fact that everyone there was my sister and my brother; I decided to try to manage the tightrope before me. Perhaps I could find spiritual harmony in this group. I longed for communion with something familiar. Though the choice was fraught with wild swings of emotions, I withstood the storm and stayed. I was determined to make peace with the past.

About a month after my arrival, I took a first step and walked up to the altar one Sunday morning to ask for prayer. The pastor's wife welcomed me there and she asked a familiar question, "Have you accepted Jesus Christ as your personal savior?"

That instantly pissed me off. Since when was that a condition of receiving prayer? I wanted to ask. I stammered and stuttered, and looked for an answer that would seem fitting, short of saying, "No."

She didn't wait and asked another question: "Who are you? I see spirits surrounding you."

I stared back blankly and asked, "Can't we just pray?" I shifted from one foot to the other as she called the pastor over.

He joined us and studied my face, my eyes, and quietly declared, "It's not of God."

Not of God, I thought. I pulled at the waist of my blue floral print dress, which was feeling tight, and I could barely feel myself breathing.

The following Thursday, I met with the assistant pastor in his office for a counseling session. Sitting with the white computer table between us, we began talking about the renewing and cleansing of the mind. I was relieved to see that they recognized the importance of clear mind, releasing the useless clutter that impedes communion with the Divine.

Ignoring what had been said to me the previous Sunday, I still wanted to make a distinction between the beliefs here and the narrow beliefs of the church of my youth. So, under the delusion that these *Americanos* would apply at least a more expansive interpretation of the Bible, I cautiously opened the subject.

"I've studied Buddhism, and I see in it some similarities to what you're saying," I said, testing the waters. "What's the difference between meditating and praying the Christian way?"

"Jesus," he answered.

I wanted to trust him with my spiritual path, so I took the risk and said to him, "The truth is, I'm Indian at heart. There beats a spirit in me that speaks to me of the grandeur of nature and the universe formed by God."

"I've sensed something different about you," he said. "My wife and I were talking about it last night."

He made no mention of having consulted with the head pastor, and I made no mention of what the head pastor had said to me. Also, though thinking it grandiose to call myself a medicine woman, I did hint that I had a medicine bag.

"We can pray for you," he said, taking out the Bible. He then read scripture from Exodus where the people brought their idols and precious jewels and presented them to the One True God as offerings. He said he could gather a group of strong believers, and I could give my medicine bag to God—meaning, I could burn the bag and all its contents.

This sounded too extreme; the idea of purification by fire. I was looking for dramatic change, but this was going too far. Perhaps there was an easier, simpler way to redemption. But could the fact I had abandoned Jesus explain the rejection I had experienced over the years? The church of my youth, and even my parents, had given up on me; the scars of having lived with different families still tormented me; my failed marriage; everything I attempted to create seemed to have scattered and been lost.

Then, there were the racial issues that kept creeping into my life. Many times I had been the lowest paid in offices. My employers would quibble over a five-dollar raise and when I quit, hire a Caucasian twenty-five dollars above my ending salary.

I experienced other subtle rejections for which I found no logical explanation; I couldn't blame it all on "them." I reasoned that the problem had to be within myself.

But in this church, I had come up against this wall yet again, and I needed to come to terms with whatever the inner disturbance was. *Not of God,* he had said. As I saw it, my part was to be willing to walk on coals if need be.

For several weeks, I struggled with the assistant pastor's suggestion that we have a prayer session to release me from the evil that surrounded me. Conscious that this would be a repetition of the history of my people, in which European Christian invaders had demanded they give up their own religion, I abhorred the idea of turning my possessions over for burning. My ancestors had had no choice in the matter, and now I was contemplating on participating voluntarily. I had to find the source of my dismay, so I drew toward the fire.

Love

On the mind/body integration front, the time finally came when I had no other choice but to confront the flashbacks I've reported earlier in my story. These flashbacks related to the first foster home I lived in. I again saw myself as a six-year-old standing at the kitchen window watching the sun scatter its orange light at the end of my first day away from home. That lonely child had followed me wherever I'd gone. Anger and resentments weighed heavily in my heart, and I was aware of a struggle between love and fear.

Throughout the journals, my dreams told about the ideal life I could live if I chose to go beyond duality. I had at least three dreams between 1980 and 1995 that offered interesting alternatives. These dreams were mere flashes of insight that, had I been "asleep," would have blended with those dreams that had succeeded in their struggle to be forgotten. These were influenced by my study of the book, *A Course in Miracles*,[94] by my work at the Center for Attitudinal Healing that was based on principles of the course, and by the meditation practices at the Nyingma Institute. My spiritual practices had given me a philosophy by which to live, and the dreams had integrated them into my psyche. I saw these rays of hope as prescriptions for happiness that someday I might fully achieve.

The first of these dreams came in 1982, and under the topic of happiness, taught me about commitment to my spiritual growth, non-judgment, and unconditional love.

The Sarape Artist

I meet a man who teaches me the importance of consistency in love and creative endeavor. He is an artist who makes colorful magical sarapes. He works on his art everyday—rain or shine, and he loves his "children" dearly.

Our encounter lasts a mere millisecond; I don't know where I am or how I've gotten here, somewhere in the cosmos. As though he has thrown a ball at me, I catch his message in my left hand. There are no words, only the certainty that he has taught me something invaluable for my waking life.

Something in this dream teaches me about discipline and the preciousness of relationship to the family, self, art, community, and all of life. It impressed upon me that trust, happiness, and love require gentleness, patience, and consistency. The artist's philosophy was subtly presenting a model for respect that I could follow. However, at the time, responsibility and even loyalty were far-off burdens that I wanted to ignore.

In the following dream, simplistic in its message, Grandmother suggests I learn to love. I had this dream the same year—1984—that she appeared to me this side of reality. This was merely a snappy, quick insight I remembered in the morning as I was entering dreams into my journal.

Whisper

Whispering into my ear she says, "If you want love, you must be willing to give it first."

Specific in its suggestion that I adjust my approach, the dream tells me to soften my heart, and bend a little. The notion of extending a hand first seemed logical, but it was too early for me. First, I needed to cleanse the darkness, a formidable undertaking, but "Whisper" did rankle me out of my lethargy and kept bothering like a persistent fly at the dinner table.

In 1990, I had the third dream that struck my curiosity with its suggestion that I be happy. Me, happy? I wondered. The dream was clear in its message, but I was yet spiritually too dense to let it seep into my waking life.

Be Happy

I lean over the nozzle, pumping gas into my blue Mercedes, when I hear the commotion of a procession like a Mardi Gras—tambourines, drums, and singing in Spanish. Looking up, I see people carrying green and purple banners, bright red ribbons, and flags waving in the breeze. A tall thin man in a refined brown suit leads the procession, and I surmise that he is their spiritual leader.

Seizing the moment, I leave the pump and fly in their direction to have a closer look. Alighting in front of the teacher, I begin skipping backward to keep ahead of the group. Up close, no distinguishing features tell me his age. He can be forty as easily as sixty or older. He reminds me of a handsome Mexican man I had once seen at Justin Hermann Plaza in my waking life. His thick black hair is slicked back; he has a regal Indian nose. His skin is smooth and clear. When I look into his eyes, I see the universe reflected in the dark of his pupils—pinpoints of light.

"Tell me what the secret of life is," I ask, shouting above the music.

"Be happy," he answers simply, and smiles.

That's it? I think. Nothing about a professional license, buying a house, or staying with the same man?

"No," he says, reading my thoughts, "be happy."

Over the years, attachment to lover, marriage, and friends, evaded me. I struggled with addictions and depression. A medical crisis was subtly eroding my ability to make sound decisions. The idea of being happy seemed like a frothy, distant notion.

These three dreams set a posture I could take in living my life from within. I needed to heal the pain of abandonment, resentments and judgments that I wore as protective armor in my clumsy efforts to find love. Nevertheless, the dreams served as pink-lens filters to dissipate the darkness of that period.

Fear

In my journals, I found numerous examples of duality: separation from God, separation from people, memories of failures, a stranger to myself. The example that most clearly illustrated the internal rift was the dream that follows. It showed me that I had opposites reflected within me in two medicine women: Aurora the teacher with a committed following, and Gracia, a poor woman with a tormented and twisted heart. Psychological homelessness was fragmenting my life, and transcending duality was the answer. The lessons I was learning in my waking state advised me to take a stand between love and fear.

Aurora y Gracia

Light filtering through the stained-glass windows, a hush falls upon the congregation as Aurora steps forward to present her teaching. She is a petite woman with long, dark hair and eyes that penetrate to the soul. She is known for her wisdom and kindness, having chosen her own name as a child because it recalled to her the beauty and spaciousness of the heavens—the beginning. In her lovely, hot pink dress, she stands at the center of the platform.

The temple, an amphitheater with a dome several stories up, is packed from the closest seats in front to the farthest ones on the first, second, and third balconies. She begins her discussion, and just when she utters her first words, a commotion is heard from the "standing-room only" area.

A woman with long, wild hair shouts at no one in particular, "Tell me! Tell me!" Her dirt-stained arms flailing about furiously, she runs down the aisle toward the front and pauses for a second before Aurora.

"Why haven't the gods been consulted?"

The voices within her clamor, and she shouts louder, "Just answer me, damn it; why weren't the gods consulted?" She stops between the front row and the platform below the black-gowned grandmothers who stand in the box seats nearby.

Why don't they just shut her up? I think.

Whether Aurora was able to finish her presentation or not, I don't recall. I did find out later that the troubled woman's name is Gracia, and that she once had the potential for being a powerful medicine woman. It isn't clear to me whether the grandmothers were the gods or whether they would consider her question and deliberate amongst themselves to offer a response.

In any event, it came to be known that it was my responsibility to figure out the source of Gracia's rage and find a way to appease her.

The contrast is shown between the priestess and the wild woman, my spiritual development and the personal demons that plagued me. At one end of the spectrum is a wise, compassionate, and developed teacher living her destiny; while at the other is a woman full of rage and disillusionment. Aurora, who chose her name as a child for its symbolic meaning—the beginning, the light, the dawn, Corn Woman—is an evolved spiritual teacher, a medicine woman passing on the teachings of the past. In the opening scene, Aurora is standing before the congregation ready to speak; and Gracia, who has suffered the defeat of missing her ultimate calling to live as a medicine woman, is flailing about furiously.

In the midst of the two opposites, stand the gods, the grandmothers: gods—beings of compassion. In her plea to them, I wondered if Gracia is not lamenting a cultural loss, loss of family, or loss of focus, but certainly, I eventually concluded, the disfavor she felt was a sharp contrast to the position held by her counterpart, Medicine Woman Aurora. Gracia had fallen far short of living her destiny, just as I had. Getting her back on track was the task of the grandmothers and Gracia herself. The path she/I must take, would lead me through the underworld byways of duality and give me a "face and heart."

This is the crux of transcending duality, or awakening, that was being offered to me: Gracia's fire burned, charred, and singed every corner of my psyche until I was totally flattened. Everything I looked at bespoke my rage; every incident, however innocent, ignited past hurts. I shouted obscenities in the most innocuous, mundane of scenes, and my face was contorted with madness. I fluctuated between listening to the promptings of the dreams of love and happiness and wanting desperately to be relieved of the fire burning within. Instead, I hung on, and whatever God's attempts at liberating me, I hung on more tenaciously to the insanity.

I insisted that there must be some process from which the *curandera*/mystic emerges to inform me that I was more significant than the dictates of life gone awry and what I had learned about myself. I had to stop living out the bitter misperceptions I had internalized from the past. I had to deal with the pain inflicted upon my family by racism and poverty. Gracia's task was to set herself free from duality and transcend it. To detach from illusion meant stepping out of the imposed confines of duality.

Whatever I endured psychologically, emotionally, physically, the role I had played in my family in my formative years, my family's economic hardships, and my own psychological homelessness were the very challenges I knew I must surmount to go beyond duality. This dream gave me a glimmer of going home. It gave me the willingness to take responsibility for my failures in life and have compassion for myself—to choose between love and fear.

Transcendence

"Going to *Tlalocan*" dream showed me that I would not have to transcend duality by myself, and that it was divine intervention that would release me. The significance of this dream took many years for me to grasp, but the imprint left by living a moment of pure consciousness was key to its message and a call that eventually moved me beyond duality. And, thus it is for all of us dreamers on a spiritual path.

Going to Tlalocan

I walk up the east side of the pyramid. At the top where everything is pristine, there is a park, beautifully tended, leaves raked, geraniums and other flowers in bloom and generously sprinkled about. The area is quiet and serene in the wee hours of the morning.

Temples at the top of the pyramid are symmetrically situated, as though to honor the path of the Sun God, a place where the shadows it throws will cast meaning onto the grounds. They stand like high-rises around a central plaza; one at the east end, the Eastern Paradise, home of warriors fallen in battle, who carry the Golden Disk midway; another at the Southern Paradise where Chalhuitliticue, Goddess of Rain, replenishes the earth and spring endures forever; a third temple stands on the west side where Mother Night blankets us with her thick, star-studded hair, and mystery awaits. House of Corn, Temple of Ciuapipiltin, home of mothers who die in childbirth, who then turn into goddesses and relieve the burden of the warriors holding the sun at midpoint and lower it to its resting place.

A fourth temple on the north stands where snow freezes, and the bitter winds howl; the nine hells of Mictlan, home of God and Goddess of Death, Totonac, and Mictlantecuhtli, where the quiet life begins its travail across wide and swift rivers, through high rugged mountains and low rocky valleys.

This is an early spring day with a slight nip in the air. The freshness uplifts and fills me with a faith and conviction that everything in my life is as perfect as it should be. I am here because I am looking for a place to live, and have an appointment with a woman to see an apartment. Conscious of the sacred surroundings, I look around to observe as closely as possible.

I walk into the vestibule of the first temple with its curved walls, cool marble floors, and a plain, round wooden table adorned by a sprig of copal burning in an urn. The woman comes out and takes me to one of the available apartments. The space is freshly painted. Even the windows sparkle and reveal a crystal clear view of an aqua blue bay below. I like the firmness of the floors, but I want something situated on the south side of the plaza.

We leave the building and enter the next temple; it houses a garden apartment facing south. We walk through the cooking area and I like it very much; the rooms are a comfortable size for me, with natural light on all sides. We nod in agreement. This is the one.

After completing our transactions, I walk back to the plaza where street musicians, vendors, and tourists are now milling about. I take a paved walkway that leads toward the center of the plaza and encounter a large brown-skinned woman who greets me by making an utterance toward me in a language I do not understand. I haven't met her before—that I can recall—but I surmise that she is telling me, "It's time you stopped acting like you are damaged goods, and started acting out of your wholeness. Walk tall, like a proud Aztec." I know she means I should stop clinging to the self-image of an abandoned child, lost and alone, that keeps me locked in depression and melancholy.

Suddenly I become awake within the dream, and I realize that I must think fast and take advantage of this exquisite moment. Nothing comes to mind but I feel an intense sadness. I take steps toward the north side, my shoulders hunched as though I'm fighting a downpour and icy wind.

I hear the woman's words again. "Stop! Stop chasing the meaningless. It's not real. You have but this instant." I feel my back straightening, tension leaving, and the lightness of the day sweeping through my consciousness. The recognition that I am air and space registers, and I experience a delightful freedom, as though I have become particles of light.

I retrace my steps to the center, away from death and toward the east, the direction from whence I came. I hear laughter and stop at a cafeteria where I come upon my friends from the Center for Attitudinal Healing having lunch. They invite me to join them.

I am glad to see them, and I sit next to Cheryl S. Then Jerry J. recognizes my voice and walks over to me and hands me a handful of small green seeds.

"I heard you are having trouble sleeping; I looked for something gentle that would help you rest," he says to me with a look of tenderness and concern.

"Thank you," I respond, extending my hand to receive his gift.

I walk back out into the bright light and begin descending the stairs. I raise my white rebozo over my head and go toward the Beginning, the home of the Rising Sun.

I think of the woman's words again, and this time I understand them differently. "Know which God you are serving, and which world you are in."

Time and space in the quadrants are so clearly marked in this dream: east-west, and north-south. Here, I see myself at the beginning of a new cycle, another round in the battle with obstacles I must overcome in my journey.

The west is a point in the cycle of life that indicates completion, as at the end of the day. West is the feminine function of creation that is held in the senses— intuition, a tool of knowing that unfolds gracefully. In the silence of darkness, commitment to Spirit is affirmed. In darkness, reality distinguishes itself, and one is attentive to its revelation under the lamp of wisdom and truth. One dares to wait or walk toward the unknown, to be in confusion or clarity, but enter into darkness, one must. Clarity comes as a result of this particular journey. Here another stage of my task to turn night into day was graciously resolving itself.

South and north make up another set of contrasts. South symbolizes birth and the fertility of the spring rains, and north symbolizes death—thus the two together symbolize a complete cycle of life. It is said that in these cycles, life and death are pieces of the God of Time, dying and being reborn. The repetition of life and death also indicates states of consciousness with similar rhythms and patterns.

It's interesting to note that my teachers at the Center for Attitudinal Healing appear in the dream, and one of them gives me a handful of "green seeds" to help me rest. In his gift, I was receiving the forgiveness I needed to extend to others and myself. Waking and sleeping were opposites, and the dreams about destiny, love, and fear needed to come together.

The process of finding my way through dimensions, thought processes, and recognizing the fine line of truth and peace, is a path that requires alertness, awareness, and a fierce determination. By choosing to overcome my judgments, heal from psychological homelessness, and overcome the obstacles on my path, a gift of consciousness had been handed to me.

This dream also showed me another contrast as spoken by the woman who greeted me at the center of the plaza. "Know which God you are serving" could mean, "Know yourself and what you have created, and be conscious of what you hold to be true, regardless of your state of being, asleep or awake." "Alert or unconscious," applies to any state of being. The task of choosing between realities was becoming apparent. I needed to choose—the God of love or the God of fear. She advised, "Know which god you are serviing ..." Was I serving the God of truth, or, was I wandering in illusion? The dream poses the question, and draws me toward the truth.

The task of awakening within the dream meant rejecting the projections and misperceptions I had accepted about reality. Just as I had struggled within dreams to be at attention, now the challenge was for me to carry truth into my waking life. By challenging the reality of my illusions—the beliefs I held about my psychological self—I could transcend duality.

A very important gift borne by this dream is revealed in the expression, "The recognition that I am air and space registers, and I experience a delightful freedom, as though I have become particles of light." This shows me the essence of our reality, an essence in which I taste expanded consciousness. The sacredness of time and space extend an opportunity to go beyond duality. I could not have learned this without the visceral sensations of becoming like particles of light. When my consciousness was impacted with a moment of truth, I experienced myself as time and space as though I had *become* particles of light.

The Old Dreamers believed that all time exists in the present moment—in the Now. This dream reminded me that I am not separate from the rest of creation. The truth about my identity is revealed, and I find that I am of one mind with all of creation in a precious union of the moment.

Remember that spiritual growth does not develop in a straight line, which is something I am emphasizing over and over; *this process took years.* I relied on community, prayer, psychotherapy, yoga, meditation, and many other disciplines. Yet, it can happen at any time. After having this dream, my life improved slowly, and I began to feel better about it.

Paradoxically, the awakening of this new consciousness occurs so subtly, so imperceptibly, that we are hardly aware of the change. This is also the moment when the lines of demarcation between the worlds dissolve, and night and day flow seamlessly into each other. The object of this task is to awaken. As we do so, we embrace and carry all of humanity in its journey toward awakening.

It's quite natural that the extended voyages into other dimensions and the work that we do in the waking state, such as meditation, yoga, or other disciplines, weaves into a tapestry of landscapes that serve to calm the spirit and the mind. This is not to say that problems don't arise, but there is a difference in the quality of change and uncertainty. You, the *curandera*, come to trust in the unfolding of life. Whatever the God of Duality has prepared for you brings about a sense of completion, and that completion reveals truth.

Prayer Heard

Eventually, I had a dream that illustrated that, with*in* the dream, I could think clearly enough to call for help. Though my earthly parents could not save me from my fate, I had the wings of awareness, the skills and tools to take myself to safety as I moved toward the realization of a deeper truth—a place where Corn Woman's teachings began to take root.

El Coyote[95]

He is as ugly as Hades, and no one is known to have escaped his grasp. Description of his physical attributes fails, because in his aura, he betrays his true being as clearly as if he emitted radio signals of his bad intent—a Bluebeard of the first caliber. He looks like a man in his late forties or early fifties, yet no one knows for sure; village memory stretches back through the centuries, and no one recalls a time when this ominous presence was absent. When he comes calling, girls are putty in his hands, and he always collects his due. Now it is my turn. The villagers are turning their backs on me, as though in a choreographed dance, leaving me to my fate.

I see his black cape and run to my mother with pleading eyes, screaming, "He's coming. He's coming." I expect her to take me to a place on the other side of the world where I will be safe and hidden. Instead, she hands me thirty-five cents in change, and says, "If you're in real trouble, call me."

"How could you?" I scream. I look at my father, and he, too, looks away. The blow is final. I feel my abductor's hot breath on my neck and his firm grip on my arm. It is time to join him, and surrender is my only option. The plaza near the bandstand is now deserted except for my parents standing helplessly by.

El Coyote grabs me with a magnetic pull backward, and when there is an opening in the trees, we begin to ascend. I jerk my arm loose, and once in the open sky, I begin to maneuver my escape. I take a nosedive, and he follows. If he is going to have me, he will have to fight me first. It seems hopeless, because he is fast and cunning. However fast I go, he moves more quickly. Fervently, with all the power of my being—for I know this as my last chance—I begin to pray, "Dios, ayudame, ayudame." "God, help me, help me." Instantly, I begin to rise at double mach speed, and instead of simply seeing the horizon, I see Mother Earth in her fullness. El Coyote's psychic hold on me weakens. He is lazy and unable to pursue any further, as though he has come to the edge of hell and the limits of his domain. I see him far below, a mere dark speck, like a deflated balloon spiraling out of control. Precious Mother Earth behind me, unfiltered light, beyond the presence that was looming over me with certain death.—Whatever the hold, I am free. I breathe deeply. I have a second chance on life.

Summary

The Old Dreamers had practices by which they guided initiates through this stage of development. As can be inferred from the old culture's relationship to nature, their complex worldview made explanation and spiritual direction absolutely necessary.

This chapter is aimed at preparing you to proceed toward transformation. In it, I attempted to illustrate the issues of psychological homeless that *curanderas/ medicine women* face. I offered psychological homelessness as an example of the challenges you may face, by using an example of my personal struggle between love and fear, to define duality in modern terms.

First, as the dreamer, you can transcend duality by stopping fluctuation of contrasts. As you define the residual feelings from your formative years, the problems will feel fixed or practically unchangeable. And secondly, behavior patterns caused by unsettling feelings, such addiction to substances, situations, types of troublesome behaviors, poor personal and professional relationships, and other issues, can be healed. You will stabilize these feelings, and find love and peace. Dreams of anguish and false identity will lead you to reclaim your true Self and reality in the sacredness of the moment—the Now. In each instant, dreams will tell you how to choose beyond duality and how to acknowledge the Divine in the present moment. Attachment to thoughts and feelings eases its grip slowly, and as it does, self-forgiveness and feelings of peace and lightness replace the internal conflicts.

Love and compassion overcome the fear that once distracted you on your spiritual path. The unraveling of your life that you agreed to on entering this journey stops here. You made a choice long ago to align yourself with truth and power

Transcendence does not happen completely on your own. Fortunately, there is always help available in our path. The woman I met at the center of the plaza reminded me that I needed to pay closer attention to the quality of my thoughts. The way I experienced myself as particles of light is a helpful reminder that our essence is beyond the body. When this type of experience happens for you, you will remember it and come back to it again and again. You will accept this consciousness and let it be emblazoned within you forever.

We humans are spirit and energy, and as such can live far beyond our earthly limitations. As you transcend duality, your consciousness expands to include perception of the forces of the universe. By interpreting your dreams in the context of the Old Dreamers, you can recognize your greatness that comes from the Creator. Corn Woman's message of transformation stems from this fountain of energy. You have the wings to soar above the suffering, and the means to explain the unexplainable through your art and medicine.

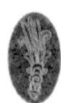

CHAPTER 10

▼

Corn Woman Sings: Initiation Completed

The Burning

In late summer of 1991, the evening of the extended prayer meeting in which I was to give my medicine bag to God, I went about my room, gathering my medicine objects: the Mexican alabaster bowl for burning copal, my silver necklace with turquoise, the amber necklace, my medicine cards, a brown leather pouch, and many other items I had seen in my dreams and gathered in my waking life. Like *La Llorona*[96] who killed her children, I was also gathering mine to sacrifice them.

I just threw them into my eagle-stenciled black bag without looking. I didn't *want* to look; I just wanted relief from the pain and disarray in my life. I threw everything I loved into the bag, but there was one thing I left out. But for now, it was time to climb the pyramid.

I arrived at the assistant pastor's house where four people were waiting for me, and a fire was burning in the fireplace. The sun was still high in the sky and shining brightly through the large window in the livingroom. I said hello to my friends, and sat down on a comfortable green velvet sofa. We began reading the Bible from Exodus. "… a jealous God … kindness to those who love me and keep my commandments."

And now the prodigal daughter was taking a step toward setting things right in the community. I took the heavy-laden bag and walked toward the fire. It was warm that evening, and the fire seemed out of place. I hesitated.

"Just throw them in," the pastor encouraged. One by one, I began. *The Course In Miracles*? I pleaded.

"Into the fire," he motioned, perhaps thinking I was backing out of the deal.

I continued … slowly … questioning my decision.

With everything cast into the fire, I returned to my place on the sofa. My skin felt tight, as though it was being stretched from the back of my neck. During the prayer I heard, "Lord, restore her." "Renew her." One by one, they each said a prayer for me.

My Return

Two or three years later, but before the "Going to Tlalocan" dream, still trapped in a quagmire of confusion, and unable to sleep one night, I got up at three o'clock in the morning, my body spent and exhausted from the agony of fluctuating between fury and illness. Writing in my journal, I had a revelation: "I am carrying this rage like a trophy, and feeling responsible for changing the world." In my mind's eye, the door to the cell in which I had locked myself fluttered between open and shut to the rhythm of my heartbeat. I was addicted to the sense of power that I felt in my hatred.

In desperation I implored, "Take this from me, God. This insanity was here before I arrived on Earth, and it will be here long after I'm gone. Help me accept peace just for this moment. Just for tonight, I want rest."

As though a dam had burst, I felt the currents of peace wash through me, and instantly, I was lifted out of my misery. I could see clearly my part in the drama. I wasn't responsible for the problems of the world. However, I *was* responsible for my part in them. As the weeks passed after that night, gradually my contact with the Divine resumed its normal ebb and flow. Without my noticing at first, I stopped dwelling on people's guilt, and eventually began to feel whole and sane again. The fullness I had experienced when I saw myself as particles of light shortly after, helped me make the final step. This was 1994.

It took time, but I made peace with the fact that the green pastures and still waters I sought were not in the answers that had served my parents. I could walk away from Christian Fundamentalism once and for all, and find my own way home. With time, I made a trip to Mexico and reconnected with my mother's family. It had been twenty-three years since my previous visit. I found *La Virgen de Guadalupe* and basked in the reverie at *La Basilica*. I felt at home. When I returned from the trip, I began to look for a rosary prayer group to join, and gradually my life found a gentle pattern that supported me. With the beat of my drum, the one item I protected from the fire, I began to feel the pulse of the community I was looking for.

This Chapter's Purpose

This segment of the dream map reveals the consciousness I found beyond duality, which appears to be what the Old Dreamers, the *Tlamitamines*, aspired to. It further illustrates why they saw the spirit world as reality and the waking world as dream. They aimed toward the heights of spiritual transformation that Corn Woman and *Quetzalcoatl* left for future generations.

First, let's illustrate the level of self-discipline the Old Dreamers demonstrated in achieving completion of their initiation and subsequent spiritual attainment. Castaneda's teacher of ten years will serve as an example: Juan Matús was a dreamer/sorcerer that entered his training in his early twenties and left it when he died sometime in his late sixties or early seventies. As described by Castaneda, his years of training included arduous mental and physical exercises that required years of practice, weeks and months of isolation in the wilderness, and adherence to strict codes of conduct that defined character of integrity and commitment.

I bring up the foregoing example to emphasize that the Old Dreamers pursued their practices as intently and methodically, and were as self-disciplined, as the Samurai of ancient Japan, or as the Tibetan ascetics who meditate in the caves of the Himalayas.

So it is with your practice; although no mountain treks or weeks of isolation in the wilderness are required for this journey, your undivided attention, self-discipline, and commitment are.

A quick review of the preconditions of spiritual attainment will assist us in putting the final stage of initiation in the context of today.

Preconditions of Spiritual Attainment

These are the definitive steps you may follow if you like in this dream map. Consciousness as explored in this chapter is met with three preconditions:

- The first is that you allow your life to unravel in order to integrate mind, body, and spirit;

- The second is that you develop awareness in your dreaming as well as your waking lives; and

- The third is that you confront and transcend duality.

After confronting duality, and facing the effects of psychological homelessness or other issues pertinent to your destiny, you may come in contact with a moment of truth that will reverberate throughout your life. Whatever your experience, it will bring you to "having a face and heart," and you now can withstand *the weight of being equal with all of creation*. One of the gifts you will receive for this journey is the knowledge that transformation is a tangible, palpable truth. If you are an experienced dreamer, you may have come to this stage through other means, and perhaps already have confronted your life's issues equal to duality.

Now we are ready to examine how the consciousness may have appeared to the Old Dreamers, and how it was revealed to me over the thirty years of dreaming.

Many Starts and Stops

Recovering the memory of our true essence has many starts and stops. From the early years of the journals, I saw flickers of light, wondered what they represented, and then was overwhelmed with other images and experiences that overshadowed the loveliness I witnessed. In my struggle with duality, I took steps forward and back many, many times.

The threads in the tapestry of my dreams would surface and then disappear into the fabric for long periods. Reemergence of the strands became more pronounced as I dealt with duality and came out the other side.

My Transformation

After the moment of awakening in the "Going to Tlalocan" dream, I went through a period of sorting through the masculine and feminine, and allowing culture to come to the forefront of my life. I began to see something new in my dreamscape. My surrender to Spirit allowed forgiveness to find a home in my heart. Forgiveness became an opening of time and space that permitted the forces of the universe to flow with relative ease.

Inquiring into the practices of the Old Dreamers, I found a connection between their pursuits and mine. Although they had many other uses for their practices, such as nagualismo, and working with the assemblage point that we spoke of back in chapter three, I realized that aspects of time and space could become allied to the practices of the dreamer in the twenty-first century. The opening of time and space, gifts of power, and transformation were precisely what the Old Dreamers desired, and this is exactly what I found that we can pursue today for empowerment. The path may be bumpy, at times even treacherous, and the pursuit of these gifts is up to you; but it's the journey that counts.

Here are further examples of how avenues of transformation can open up. For you, it need not be Corn Woman; it need not be the Sun or *Quetzalcoatl*, but there will be an opening that will reveal what you seek. The following dreams will illustrate how the shift from duality opened the door to transformation for me.

Time and Space

"I Am the Sun" is a dream that has been revealing itself to me since 1997. At first, I saw it as support to continue working on the research necessary for writing this book. When I met a priest who became my spiritual director, I concluded that the lessons his presence showed me concerned acceptance and unconditional love. As I've been working on this dream map, however, I've become aware of another level of dreaming:

"I Am The Sun" is not about "The Traveler," the original title I gave the dream. In the context of the Old Dream traditions, the *purpose* of dreaming was to *be* transformed and see oneself as imbued with aspects of creation as the Creator made us. Humans are, as the Creation Stories say, aspects of the Creator. Everything in the universe comes from the same source. Therefore, nothing is ever separate from it. Separation is impossible.

I define time and space as the quiet, calm inner world we see when we have encounters with the Divine. The silence of the dream conveys the message that we are powerful beings, reflections of our Creator. The help that the monk in the dream lends for the continuation of this project is important, but minor in comparison to the dream's main message.

I Am the Sun

Like a tumbleweed that, traveling over the road, pauses occasionally and then rolls on, he is known as a wanderer in brown robes, easily gathering people around him with his compassionate and caring manner. He's been to Paris, all over Europe, Tahiti and other places in the South Pacific, and now he is coming to Second and Hunter Streets in Stockton. I am here out of curiosity. I have never met him before, and do not know his name.

A group of friends and I gather at the Jimenez home to wait for the monk. I walk up the front stairs of the house. The door is missing, and I can tell that this little cottage has not been used for a long time. When I was a little girl, the family owned these three houses on the Second Street side of the block. All three houses are now deserted. From the porch, I scan the dusty, empty living room of the middle house and sit down. Sitting and leaning against a post, I put my elbows on my knees and cradle my face with my hands. I close my eyes. It has been weeks since I have opened the manuscript, and am feeling overwhelmed and discouraged at the volume of revision that lies ahead.

My friend Kathleen pulls up driving a silver, 1980 Cadillac Seville with the holy man riding on the passenger's side. He gets out. He is a big man, tall, with graying reddish hair and beard. The crowd closes in around him, and I hear his gentle voice and kind remarks to the friends he greets, but I keep my distance from him. He comes up the stairs and sits next to me. His soft blue eyes melt my heart, and I lean on his shoulder and revel in his love; he is a friend and a father at once. I miss my father terribly, but seeing the stranger is better than the best times I'd ever spent with him. I bask in the warmth of the monk's presence.

Shortly, the traveler announces that he will be leaving. He goes back to the car, pulls out something from the back seat, and walks toward me again.

"It's not my destiny to do anything with this manuscript. It's Simon and Schuster quality. See that it gets published," he says, handing me a package tied in a bow with white, translucent ribbon.

I read the cover letter, a long poem that sends me into reverie with feelings of wide expanses and power, as though I were hovering above the world with the sun as my torch and guiding light, with freedom to travel to other universes; beautiful feelings of joy pouring through me. I flip the pages of the manuscript to get a sense of its contents. Some checks that belong to him fall out.

"Kathleen, call him back," I shout. She is walking through the crowd in the street. "We don't even have a mailing address for him."

"He's gone already," she shouts back.

At heart, I know the checks have been left intentionally. The added gift is support and spiritual currency for the next part of the journey.

"It's not my destiny to do anything with this manuscript …" In hearing his words and being handed the text, it was as though I had been given a gift, and it *was* a gift—a gift of power—the spiritual currency to stay with the project. At the time of this dream, I was struggling to integrate the Creation Stories with the results of the formal investigation I had conducted—eight years of combing through bits and pieces of hidden history and dreams.

Shortly after the dream, I did meet the priest. His ministry was working with the homeless. As significant as the similarities between the monk in the dream and this priest were, something in me kept looking for a deeper meaning.

Finally, it occurred to me that in the sensations of power and joy I had experienced in reading the cover letter, I actually had seen emanations from the Sun.

As I pointed out back in chapter eight, today, we do not think of the Sun as capable of giving us spiritual power, nor do we see ourselves capable of receiving it either. Our ancestors took this type of experience to illustrate the vastness of our creators and their creations. As I studied the dream and came back to it many times, the sensations of exquisite joy within it finally brought the message home loud and clear: *I am an emanation from the Sun!* Our ancestors perceived the Sun as a powerful god and performed extensive rituals to honor it.

It took several more years for me to connect this dream with Corn Woman and Quetzalcoatl's message of transformation: Her message was delivered in the Creation Stories, the one in which she allowed her head to be cut off to give us hope. Quetzalcoatl's message in jumping into the fire was that he was returning home by way of fire. As Quetzalcoatl traveled through the levels deep within Earth, his journey symbolically carved out a route toward transformation through the caverns of our spiritual existence.

"I Am the Sun" also led me to see another meaning of the Mayan saying about the dream struggling against the dreamer to be forgotten. They are not only referring to our nightly dreams, but also, to the "great dream," the reality of our "true home." In our dreams, we see through the lens of the great dream, and from that perspective, we finally remember the true essence of our being.

Another Step toward Transformation

Beyond the pain and suffering of duality, time and space can connect us to true joy and peace. In the following dream, which is also an example of the consciousness the Old Dreamers sought, two important points are made about reality: what our essence is, and that there is help available to release us from duality. As healer/artist, on the alert for your own obstacles, even as you are working through issues, you will get glimpses of total perfection. In the dream "Blow the Doors Out," I take another step toward transformation with the help of a spirit being prompting me.

Blow the Doors Out

The temple is deserted when I walk in and sit down midway to the front. A dim glow shows the slight outline of engravings on two wooden panels behind the altar. As my eyes became accustomed to the light, the engravings begin to resemble Rorschach cards, but I can't decipher much more. I hear a voice from behind say to me, "Stretch your consciousness." I turn around, and see that I am alone.

I imagine what "stretch your consciousness" means, and I manage to create an awareness of space a couple of feet around me.

"No, Noni, blow the doors out."

I expand my consciousness a second time, and I hear an explosion. The roof explodes, the walls blow apart, and the floor blasts out from under me. The rubble of what had been the little box of personal space disintegrates into millions of specks, and creates a cloud of dust around me. Everything is blown into pieces, including myself, and I drift in the vast silence as pure energy.

In this dream, I receive instruction from a spirit being. The voice is encouraging me to drop the belief system about my psychological self and stretch my imagination, the lens through which I see the vastness of The Great Mystery, and of time and space. As though emphasizing the need for total surrender, the voice challenges me to completely let go. "Blow the doors out," is actually an invitation to experience a heightened state of consciousness. I am being offered an opportunity to reach far beyond duality, and the general beliefs I hold about my "self" as opposed to my true Self. This dream occurred toward the end of twenty-five years of journal keeping wherein I experience a magnificent sense of my being as pure energy—a beautiful example of the consciousness the Old Dreamers sought.

As the multidimensionality of the early cultures reaches out and impresses upon you a magnificent spaciousness and vibrant beauty, that spaciousness and beauty will blow out the doors and walls of your old concepts and leave you standing in a wonderful new place. As you examine your dreams, whatever greatness you see, embrace it, for that is the true essence of who you are. You can always trust your dreams and be guided by them.

Meeting the Feminine

In previous chapters I discussed the impact of Grandmother's presence on my concept of God. Now I present another facet of Spirit that left its particular mark late in my story, and further explains how Grandmother influenced my awakening to the feminine face of God. These dreams are spread over the twenty-five years that covered my formal investigation, and have continued since. I mention their spread to illustrate that dreams do not have an order in the progression of our spiritual development. You may have a startling revelation while in the midst of attempting to awaken in your dream life, or in the midst of your struggles with duality. They can come at any time.

Queen Announced

Throngs of people wait outside the palace, and we can hear the commotion mounting as the moment of her appearance draws near. I wait with a French woman in the queen's parlor. An enormous dark Samoan woman wearing a plain black muumuu comes from the queen's chamber and advises in a soft voice, "I am sorry you must wait so long."

Apparently, this woman has closer ties with the queen than anyone else, and is coming out to warn us that we must be patient and be ready.

"Is it all right if I read a book while we wait?" I ask.

"No, no. She prefers your full attention when she calls," she answers.

The stage was set by the announcement of the queen's soon appearance. The Samoan woman, a spirit being, requested that I be attentive in the meantime. That she was Samoan awakened me to the fact that other cultures are related to my own, but most strikingly, she, like Grandmother, strengthened my identification with the Feminine. She had a spaciousness of quality in her enormity. Somehow she awoke within me an expectation of seeing something ancient as part of the new worldview that was unfolding. I wasn't sure how to interpret her presence. In my encounter with this spirit being, I began to perceive another world to which I had previously been blind. She captured my attention, and I began to watch for something special.

A gap of about fourteen years passed between the "Queen Announced" dream and the arrival of the queen. This dream came in 1994, about a year after my leaving the Christian community.

Meeting the Queen

I met the Samoan woman when I visited the palace years ago, and waited for the queen. I remember how unprepared I was at that time. "Is it all right if I read my book?" I had asked. This time, I am at attention.

"She's on her way," the attendant announces.

A hush falls upon the room. Through the huge plate glass window, the panoramic view of green rolling hills sets the stage for her appearance. I see her rounding the corner. She floats past the window in her white flowing gown. It looks as though she is ice skating, but then I remember, of course, she doesn't need ice skates. She merely taps her foot, and glides above ground.

The door opens and I feel her energy like a soft, warm summer breeze. She comes directly toward me. "I'm so glad you're here," she says, caressing my face tenderly. I melt into her dark dancing eyes. Her lady in waiting, the Samoan woman, stands by, beaming with pride, for it is she who has groomed me for this moment.

My encounter with her is far too brief, for she announces just as suddenly as she has arrived, that she is leaving, and I am left looking at her salt and pepper braid down her back. I beg her attendant with imploring eyes, "Must she be gone so soon?"

Smiling lovingly, she reminds me, "I warned that you must be at attention. She arrives, leaves her blessing, and is gone before you know it."

In this dream, reference was made to the previous dream that announced the coming of the queen. It also indicates relationship between the Samoan woman and me: "… for it was she who has groomed me for this moment." What is fourteen years in eternity? She prepared and cleansed me for these precious moments with the Divine. The immense joy and love impressed itself on my consciousness.

"I warned that you must be at attention," also illustrates the role awareness plays in our path toward transformation. The significance of the Samoan woman and her message that I must be alert is as important as the blessing received.

Finding Lost Years Again

I remember the days of coming back to *La Virgen*. My first memories of her are centered in the summer vacations we took to Mexico, when I visited the beautiful colonial churches and the Sunday crowded plazas. I recall the first time I saw her image; I was with my mother's cousin Josefina at the old Basílica. Now when I look back, I think of those days with longing and nostalgia.

When I went to the Mission bookstore in San Rafael to buy my first book of rosaries, I picked up other items, and the tall slender young man behind the counter totaled them up. "That will be $12.12," he said. I looked up from my checkbook to see if he was joking, but the inside joke didn't seem to register with him. Apparently, it was just between her and me. Her birthday is celebrated on December 12.

It's been forty-five years since my mother died. With time, my relationship with her healed. She's more human to me now. It was the dream stories, however, that changed me. Through Grandmother's tutelage, the tutelage of the spirit of *La Virgen de Guadalupe*, I've come to see *La Madre*, The Mother, as my true mother. For one who felt so unworthy, receiving her love and compassion has been a gift of immense magnitude that has filled a vast emptiness.

The following dream that I had in about 1995 illustrates the sacred love I have come to cherish from the Mother.

Madre

Four-year old Noni feels irritable and nothing Mother offers satisfies her.
"¿Jugo? (Do you want some juice?)"
Mother sits at a 1950s' gray dinette table, almost miniaturizing it by her size, Noni is standing between her legs while I stand nearby, leaning against the bright yellow kitchen wall and watching. The sun shines through the sheer curtains. It is morning, and the air feels warm and embracing. I feel as if the nectar of the gods is flowing through me by my being in her presence.
"No," says the little one, and shyly hides her face in Mother's breasts.
"¿Tienes hambre? (Are you hungry?)"
"No," she says with a tone of exasperation.
Mother, an Indian woman with broad hips and voluptuous full breasts, recognizes that the only thing the child really needs is rest and love. Noni is well beyond nursing age, but Mother knows. She knows what the child needs. Tenderly picking up the child as though lifting a delicate porcelain vase and setting the child on her round, soft lap, Mother brings her huge breast out of her blouse and puts it in the child's mouth. Mother is so large, I have to bend over to make sure the nipple is in the child's mouth. I nod.
Mother was right. The child immediately settles down and goes to sleep peacefully.

This dream adds to the thread of dreams about the Mother that reawakened in me my love for her. The dream itself takes place in our home kitchen on Hunter Street in Stockton, California. I am both four-year Noni and the girl of fifteen years standing by. In between the dream years in my waking life, I had been shifted between numerous foster homes, and the kitchen was my mother's kitchen, a place that held both happy and sad memories. Though in my waking life, I was into my early fifties, the sacredness of the dream moment gave me back those now distant years.

It is difficult to summarize the effects of time and space in a few sentences. But, what can be said in simple terms is that time and space occurs in the awareness and silence of the breath, and requires a finely-tuned ear and amplified sensory nerves to receive its message. There is only Now; how we make up for the lost moments of life and love, it matters little as long as we believe it is possible.

Nagualismo

Now, continuing along another avenue toward transformation as seen in the old cultures, I return to the subject of nagualismo in order to demonstrate its role in breaking through duality.

In the chapter on the aliveness of nature, I discuss a dream about Mother Bear. I saw her and her cub scavenging through garbage cans, and I heard a voice say that the bear and her cub had lost their way because the environment had changed so much. At the time, I was just starting Autogenic Training, and I wondered what in me was changing, and whether, in fact, there was something I should know about the consciousness of the bear.

In this next dream, "Spinning," we get the remainder of the story and see what the cultures have lost in forgetting the consciousness she rekindles.

First, it is a lesson on the sacredness of the bear, and secondly, in nagualismo or shape-shifting. In my investigation I found the ties that bind us to the spirit of the bear (and all of nature) are vital to the well-being of the human race. In the "Spinning" dream, its aliveness is reawakened for me with the suggestion of using it as a vehicle for transformation. Keep in mind that all of creation is united and that inclusion of all consciousness is vital for its completion. The spirit of the bear can guide us on our path toward transformation.

Spinning

My friends and I talk and laugh casually, walking through a woodsy, sparsely populated area, when we come upon her. At first we see only a tree trunk with a bear's face carved into it. No one thinks anything of it until I look closer and discover her gentle feminine spirit smiling back.

"What a beautiful smile," I comment to the others. She looks at me and then turns her eyes to see who else is with me. Her eyes sparkle with delight at seeing us gathered around her. I step closer to her and move my hand toward her nostrils so that she can sense me. She kisses my knuckles, and with a twinkle and a wink of her eyes, thanks me for introducing myself.

As she peruses the situation, she realizes that no one seems to recognize who she is. Suddenly, she stands up and we have a full view. Her torso is shaped and carved from a strong tree trunk. Spinning so fast that only a blur is discernible, and with a speed that terrifies and stuns us, she transforms herself into a sixteen-year-old girl and joins a couple going into town for dinner.

I wonder whether the couple knows her true identity and the company they are keeping.

When I began the journals, my consciousness of Bear Spirit was frozen, and so it was in this dream. When I first see her, the spirit of the bear appears as though in a petrified state, a face carved into the trunk of a tree. By introducing myself, it is as though I am attempting to reawaken consciousness as the Old Dreamers perceived it. Also, as I previously said about smiles, the smile conveyed a state of consciousness that I had begun to recognize as sacred. This feeling was important, because it captured my attention and awakened me to the present moment.

An important issue in this dream is that the bear appears again to point the way to awareness of its sacredness. She became highly annoyed that we were not cognizant of her identity. Her presence caused me to wonder. Now, of course, it is obvious: *the bear is calling our culture to stand at attention in the presence of all of creation.* The point is to have reverence for all of life—nature, feminine/masculine, animals, and earth, air, fire, and water.

As mentioned previously, the practices the Old Dreamers used for shape-shifting are now focused on transformation. Manipulation of the assemblage point was a more accessible avenue for shape-shifting. Still, within a dream, spinning is a significant aspect of metamorphosis. The Old Dreamers perceived spinning in any dream as *energy that beckoned the dreamer to duplicate it*; either in her waking or dreaming states. The spinning was the key that symbolized the dropping away—shaking, perhaps, of all that was superfluous, for in this state, only the spiritual has value.

The spinning, for me, created sensations of awakening. The sensations that these types of invigorating dreams stir within lift the dreamer, and contact with Spirit takes us to another level in relationship with all of creation. In the old traditions, the dreamers may have practiced spinning in the waking state, in an effort to duplicate it and so achieve metamorphosis. But certainly, it was the increased consciousness that was the object of adoration and achievement.

Recognizing the oneness of All of Life, the practice of transforming oneself into other species, existed not only in Mesoamerica, but in many other parts of the Americas.[97] This illustrates how humans and nature are interrelated. What seems apparent is the fact that dreamers, understanding their true nature and "home," live their lives from the perspective of their dreams and practice at bringing those worlds into the material plane.

But, if we examine spinning under the microscope, we find that it's Time, Space, and the Four Directions that hold the Wisdom of the Ages.

Awakening to the memory is necessary to understand the idea of nagualismo or shape-shifting. Fortunately, the awakening does not occur in a vacuum. As we've seen, destiny, empowerment, and spirit beings ensure that dreamers are set aright on their path of transformation. From these rays of light, the world of the dreamer is rendered as one. The charge we get from within alerts us to the aliveness of nature, and dreams turn us to stand at attention and reach beyond duality.

Transmutation, changing a substance into something else, and metamorphosis, changing oneself into another form, are ways to move from having power *over* people, to having power *with*, reaching for the ultimate of liberation and reunion with the Divine. The growth and development of power was crucial to manifestation of a supernatural order, and power was the means used for attaining that union with the Divine.

Threads in the Tapestry

To conclude these thoughts about nagualismo, I found that avenues of transformation in the old cultures, such as meetings with the feminine and nagualismo, were distinct in the content of their messages. They led me to form a new relationship with the Divine, as well as impressing upon me a new awareness of my relationship with all of creation. But, as mentioned in chapter one, dreaming is a tapestry of threads that come together to create a new consciousness. The purpose of dreaming—the place where all these avenues toward transformation come together—is also to still the mind, to help us pause, witness the magnificence of creation, and come face-to-face with the Divine.

For me, it wasn't until after my struggles with duality that these aspects of dreaming began to come into focus. Just as we mature spiritually in our meditative life, dreaming also plays a vital role in our spiritual evolvement. When those moments of consciousness occur and we see truth, even if for only a moment, our consciousness is awakened, and we begin to look for the connecting threads that make all of creation one body of reality.

We are not our bodies. However, in the relaxation of the mind and body, we settle into deeper levels of awareness that bring us closer to the truth of who we are. As we clear out the obstructions from our mind, we free-fall multidimensionally and find safety and truth. In the end, we realize that there is no distinction between nature, humans, and the Divine.

Eternal

We come now to the end of my story and the closing of its circle. In a dictionary of myths and legends I found that,[98] the complexity and intertwining of North American stories of eagle and Corn Woman provide the foundation of numerous ceremonies and societies that empower with the gift of healing and perpetuation of life. The eagle's appearance often symbolizes the completion of initiation, and is similar to the Mesoamerican belief in The Feathered Serpent (Quetzalcoatl) as symbol of transformation.

While I have been discussing the sacredness of spirit beings, nature, and other aspects of reality throughout this dream map, on another level, I have been referring to the process of bringing mind, body, and spirit together as a means of expanding awareness and developing the ability to hold still as the magnificence of the eternal comes into view. Now we are taking another step off the precipice for an encounter of a different sort—an encounter that is in a category unmistakably its own.

The following dreams occurred in 1995, almost twenty years into the journals, and have a quality of completion.

The Eagle

I walk up a mountain with a group of people. We are on retreat in the desert.

The flap of a bird's wings makes us duck quickly as it flies overhead. I glance upward and see that it has a tremendous wingspan that diminishes us by comparison, and makes the bird look as large as an airplane. The beauty of its silver-tipped feathers is so spectacular that we spontaneously sigh an "ahh" that reverberates off the mountain and bounces across the valley floor to the mesas miles away.

At first I think it is an owl, and then I see that it is an eagle. An eagle!

He alights on the boulder just a few feet away from us. I tilt my head back to see his full height. He adjusts his wings majestically at his sides and looks at me. His dark eye tells me he is there for a reason—for us to drink in the wonder of his splendor. We can't help but behold him and revel in his royal presence.

The flap of the eagle's wings is a call to consciousness. Always when something sacred is happening in my dreams, a sound or energy brings me to attention, and the flap of the eagle's wings had a distinct sound that instantly alerted me. Also, the beauty of the wings, and the "dark eye," engaged me further to come to attention. This dream's message told me that I must choose between consciousness and sleep. Should I choose to awaken, I could attain the power to enter into the wholeness of our existence.

The "Eagle's Gift" as Castaneda[99] called it, is the consciousness to recognize the meaningless path of duality or illusion. One can choose a state of alertness in the moment—a moment that is filled with a magnificent expansion of time, space, and eternity, as though the gods of the universe were embracing one.

There are no earthly words to describe it. This is the moment the Old Dreamers prepared for throughout their lives—the moment in which they could witness the expansiveness of the universe. That was what I witnessed.

Over the centuries, Corn Woman has evolved into many goddesses throughout the Americas: Thought Woman; Spider Woman; She Who Created Maize (the main staple of the people); She, the Protectoress and Nurturer of the People, the Provider of Sustenance. In the Mesoamericas, she is *Omeccihuatl, Coatlicue, Tonantzín, La Virgen de Guadalupe* who created the stars and the universe, who is absolver of our human errors; the same goddess incorporated into the Catholic Church as La Virgen de Guadalupe, our Mother of Compassion.[100] She is the ancient voice that sings softly, whispers, coos, and calls us to awaken.

Corn Woman Sings

I live in the Arizona desert where sagebrush grows wild and fragrant, and the majestic tall, mature saguaros grow in abundance. In the distance, red mesas stand powerful and timeless. A film crew made up of several Asian, Mexican, and Native American students comes to document Corn Woman's Life.

She stands facing the sun with a gentle breeze blowing through her waist-length hair and the soft blue gown she wears. She is breathtaking in a blend of features that evince compassion, love, and tenderness. Standing behind her, I feel as though I hold the power of eternity in my hands, and the sound of a choir of a thousand angels singing fills my being with currents of wondrous joy.

The director, a stocky middle-aged Mexican man with dark skin and black wavy hair signals for cameras to get ready. A hush falls over the group, an indescribable sense of creation in the Six Directions—the east, the west, the north, the south, above and below. Cameras begin rolling.

Corn Woman's love for her children pours forth from her being like ribbons of smooth, silky energy. Her thoughts feel like the colors and the light of dawn, a spectacular array of the morning light. She sings of the beauty of the stars and Grandfather Sun, of the wisdom of Grandmother Moon, and of the depth and spirit of Mother Ocean.

She sings, and we become spirit, infinite. She sings and we become the vastness of the universe and see the wonder of the Great Mystery.

Corn Woman's love pouring out like silky energy and her thoughts, emanating like colors of the dawn, convey feelings of unity; the unity in the universe where Masculine dances with Feminine, and together they create the dual-gender god of the ancestors; the unity where time and space become one with everything, and pulsate in rhythm to the symphony of the universe, announcing all as one; all as sacred.

In becoming infinite spirit, we find the supreme consciousness of the Old Dreamers that empowered them to transcend duality, and come face-to-face with the Ultimate. They understood that greatness lay in becoming nothing in order to become All. When this happens for us, we cannot crawl back into our shells; we then know also that something within has reached its completion, and made space for a new cycle of growth.

Summary

As I close the final chapter, I give thanks to our ancestors for their commitment and devotion in their practices. The stories and legends they left for us continue to guide and give us direction on our paths toward transformation. Their love for the divine and sacred touches and moves me to the depths of my being. Their foresight, preparation, and the sacrifice they made in saving from destruction what they could are an invaluable gift to us. I'm sure they are watching our progress.

The power of creation and the forces that lead us toward transformation flow indiscriminately. It simply is. It neither pushes nor resists. Corn Woman's call to awaken is one of the signposts the Old Dreamers left for us to follow. To understand their world, we as dreamers must transcend duality. In pursuing avenues for transformation, such as time and space, nagualismo, and meetings with the Divine, we encounter that light, the power of creation, from which all of life flows, and we realize that we are not separate in this aspect of creation. As we accept this truth, we find happiness and peace. "Beginning," "Dawn," "Light," and "Corn," all come from the same Quiche word,[101] and we humans are of that. After the unraveling of our lives, becoming awake within our dreams, and moving through duality, we welcome the new day united with the forces of creation.

Today, purification by fire is symbolic; we purify ourselves by burning copal, sage or other sacred herbs. The smoke purifies our spirit and makes way for the Divine to appear. We recognize the Divine in all of nature and time and space. We cherish the silence because we know that therein lives the sacred.

Each day, our prayer begins with thanks to the Grandfather of the east, the Beginning, Grandfather Sun, for the life, light and warmth that is given to us, and the new opportunity to serve. We also give thanks to the Grandfather of the north. Winter and death are where yesterday ceases to exist. We die to begin anew, and we have only this moment. We can choose each moment where to focus our attention. We give thanks to the west for Grandmother Night who blankets us with faith, courage, and wisdom to enter into the unknown and the Great Mystery. Finally, we give thanks to the south, where spring rains fertilize the seed and bring forth new life and the sustenance and nurturance we need for our journey. The curtain is pulled back. As it is in other dimensions, so it is manifest here. We live moment by moment as though we are born afresh with each breath. No moment like any before. Only Now.

When you have tasted the expansiveness of truth, at the end of the day you can lay your head down to rest, anticipate reunification with All That Is, and become one with It. Gifts of power come in your relationship with the Creator; in the spaces within creation, and in the forces and powers that create light and confirm that in reality we are made by and of the Creator. Remember that in letting yourself become transparent, you find All. Greatness lies in dissolving and blending with All That Is, and allowing yourself to be used in its service. In the end, you will appreciate the fact that you have been given everything you need.

These are the prayers Corn Woman chants to us in our dreams, and whispers to us in every breath we take to awaken and find the Everlasting.

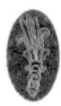

C H A P T E R   11

▼

Conclusion

This book has been thirty years in the writing. The drive for this project has come from a mixture of motives. One was to follow the directive from the elders in my dreams—to leave a piece of work that will empower future generations. The other was the desire to leave behind a map to explain our dreams from an indigenous perspective—a perspective in which we are using our own creation stories. In short, I wanted others to bypass the confusion of psychological homelessness.

Our early religions would work just fine for us if we could only remember them. I needed to understand my culture. The seed the elders planted in me was a desire to find out what, from our past, defines who we are as Chicana/o *curanderas*, mystics, and artists.

Living in a culture that relies heavily on science and decries the realms of the spirit, how else will we define our reality?

Destiny has been like a persistent lover; courting, teasing, and ever drawing me forward. But along with the unpredictable, erratic, and extraordinary experiences within my dreams, great rays of hope touched other aspects of my life, and I felt called to do something for which I could find no explanation. In the end, I found a name for it—The Beginning, Dawn, Corn Woman, The Near and Close.

However, I have one more dream I must tell you.

La Mujer Dichosa
(A Lucky Woman)

I'm walking along a tree-lined sidewalk, in a neighborhood of elegant houses when I see light flicker off something shiny hidden in the grass. I bend over to pick it up and discover a beautiful golden ring covered with mud. I clean it off with the sleeve of my black sweater and throw it up in the air, catching it with my right hand and thinking, "I'm such a lucky girl."

The journey has been far from easy going, and it is not about being lucky, but about being grateful. It always seemed that I was one step behind the rest of the world, starting projects when my peers were finishing theirs. At fifty-four, I began work on my doctorate and finished it despite poor health. Then I saw that the dissertation needed to be placed in a context that could be understood by people of our culture. That was hard, but if asked to do it again—in a heartbeat—yes, of course.

The journey of dreaming, writing, research and investigation gave me another benefit: in exploring our cultural history, I discovered the inconsistencies within my own life and the way I was choosing to live it. And coming to terms with it, my culture, my destiny, and my name, I had to come to terms with my relationship to my family as well. Looking back, the gift was about claiming all of these aspects of life and walking the road with dignity.

I also discovered two medicine women, Aurora who was self-possessed and calm, and Gracia, frustrated and fearful, who kept my life in disarray. In healing Gracia, I came to understand the significance of Aurora.

At various points, I thought changing my name would be necessary rather than pretend to have ownership of a name that had so much history in the family. I discovered that the name Ellie, which is a name that was given me spontaneously when I took my first job in San Francisco, also means light. I like the ring of that name too, and have come to appreciate my name with time.

An Invitation

In closing, I leave you with these *consejitos*, or parting words.

Comadre, Compadre, I invite you too to dip your ladle into the Milky Way and bring forth your sacred gifts. Throw caution and modesty to the wind. Use them, and let their expression be seen in your life in a way that brings you to the truth of who you are.

This dream map supports your making a commitment to your life. If your life is worth living, it's worth letting Corn Woman be the director. The stories the Old Dreamers left point the way for us today. Letting your life slowly unravel will present many difficulties, but then, is the river of life ever just a smooth sail? Developing awareness and the other gifts that unraveling brings is vital in our early steps toward awakening. Coming into relationship with the spirit world stretches awareness of that world into our waking lives.

Your bond with nature is also a result of that first commitment—the commitment to be in relationship to that world. This relationship will help you put things in perspective, for being in relationship with nature also helps you define your path. Our Native American brothers and sisters have a reason for referring to the elements of nature as "*all our relatives.*" The ability to face your fears in your dreams, and make the other choices you will need to make, comes as a result of courage and the support you receive from trees, rivers, fresh air, the sky, and all other natural things. There is no end to the level of support available to you as your awareness expands and you allow yourself to receive guidance from our relatives in nature. You will see.

When faced with duality and choosing to go beyond it, you assure your way home. Your dreams will guide you in making these important decisions that life puts in your path. You have a song to sing, so sing it out. As a *curandera*/writer/healer/shape shifter/mystic, take the gifts that resonate best for you, and expose them to the light of day. This process will take you toward transcending duality, and choosing to transcend duality is the single most significant decision you will ever make. All aspects of life are interrelated with it.

Belt It Out

If you are a writer or storyteller, connect your gifts to the old stories that are locked delicately on the shelves of universities, libraries, and in the history of your family. Record them, publish them, and tell them over and over to your heart's content.

Take your family's history and transform it into the magic that will empower your life and lead you to a truer and deeper understanding of your human existence. Investigate, and become a self-taught cultural anthropologist. Tell us about your findings. You are a *curandera*, and that's what we *curanderas* do.

Blast your music out. Dance it, and ask others to join you in the celebration of life. Our ancestors based their culture on ceremony, song, and poetry. When we dance and sing, we honor their memory and carry forth their dream of life. They know we're happy because they live in our dreams.

When we splash our paintings onto public buildings, our homes, and our schools, we enliven the world with the wonder of infinity as *they* lived it. This also gives our communities the symbols that remind us of who we are.

Thinking of the hardships our ancestors went through in having their temples demolished and their gods desecrated, I think of the levels of transformation they went through, and the stretching of their world as they initially thought it to be.

When people move up to *El Norte,* so it is with them, and so it is with you. You face these same hardships and the same opportunity for transformation. Destiny asks us to open up even the smallest parts of ourselves to be renewed. Bringing forth gifts of power is precisely what one does to transcend duality. Let go, and let power grow.

In this dream map, we have seen the power that the ancient dreamers used to shape-shift and transform matter. When you look closely at how you do it in your life, you will find that there is finesse to your methods. Stories today indicate that people can make dramatic transformations, but as conscious *curanderas/* dreamers, and mystics, we don't need to be dramatic. What we need to do is dare to be seen, and to support one another in our art, enrich our culture, and leave traditions for the next Seven Generations. Exploring your dreams, discovering your destiny, and putting this process into practice: these are your tasks.

The power of the past will manifest through you. The year 2011 is upon us. The return of the consciousness our ancestors anticipated is now. Receive it easily and effortlessly. You can do it. You know how.

The mind spins, spins, and spins. If the spinning remains undirected, power is diffused and scattered. Entering the world of your dreams enables the mind to slow down, and you find the wisdom of the ages available to you. You find spaces between the spaces. Meditating on the Four Directions: east, north, west, south, and also on above and below, you will find the secrets of the universe revealed to you. Take your time; do it slowly; open your eyes between the breaths; you will receive what you need. Slow the mind down and stay focused.

My Work on these Pages Is Done

The dream map is finished. It's my legacy to you, *Comadre/compadre.* I can say about destiny and power that they have held me together when I felt completely conquered. I have finally learned that I am ever free, that I belong, and that I am home at last. Home is a mansion of many dimensions, sacred gifts, and endless power.

I now have good health, my marriage of almost fifteen years is stable and happy, and we have a home. I've seen that the little things count most in life: home, a smile, touch, red roses in bloom, a chirping sparrow, the pink rays of sunrise, family, friends, commitment, community, and a place to meditate.

It's time for the next generation to add to this dream map, to challenge it or to modify it. This is only one *curandera's* story, and there will be many, many more.

Always remember that Corn Woman's spirit, the power of the universe that leads us toward transformation, is alive and very available. Court her; invite her to dance with you. Sing your song. Greatness longs to be in relationship with you. Use your power wisely, share it generously, and be happy.

Epilogue

"Josefina? Pepita, habla Leonor—Josefina, this is Leonor," I said.

"Leonor?" she asked, pausing a moment.

"Si," I answered.

"Pero mira nomás, muchacha. ¿Cuanto tiempo hace?—I can't believe it. How long has it been?"

"Veinte y tres años—twenty-three years," I answered

This was no impulsive call to Mexico City, but the fulfillment of my intention to reconnect with her, a yearning to see and hold her, a longing that had been growing steadily. She was my mother's first cousin, and I had thought that perhaps I was too late. She was eighty-three years old, and it had been years since our last contact.

We chatted briefly. Her husband had died when he was ninety—they had moved from Guillermo Prieto in the Santa María District. My mother's only remaining sister had died in 1987; all the other aunts from my mother's generation had died; my cousin Rosalina had moved to Guadalajara eighteen years before; and another cousin's children were graduating from the university. There were even *great* grandchildren.

"*Siento que estoy despertando*—I feel as if I'm waking up," I said.

"*¿Como dices?*—What do you mean?" she asked.

"*Pués, no se. No se porque me alejé de tí, y porqué no he ido a Mexico por tanto tiempo, pero siento que estoy despertando y que tengo muchas ganas de volver.*—I'm not sure why I distanced myself from you, from Mexico, but I have a strong desire to return, and to see you."

"*Ven pronto. Ya estoy vieja. Ya sabes que aquí tienes tu casa.*—Come soon. I'm old now. You know you always have your home here."

"*Sí, gracias,*" I said. "*Lo voy a pensar*—Yes, I will think about it."

I missed her deeply. As if coming out of a dream, I yearned to see and be with her. She invited me to come to Mexico City for a visit, and I said I would think about it. I hung up the phone. It was the summer of 1998, and I still had six weeks of vacation left. I'm going, I decided. Within forty-eight hours, I had my plane ticket, and I was ready.

Homecoming

I took one last look at my empty apartment: the glossy dark hardwood floors were dusted and all that was left were the memories of my recent past. The door shut softly behind me for the last time, and I walked to the end of the hall and stepped into the rickety elevator cage. I heard the cables shaking as I went down three floors to the street.

By the time I reached the loading area at the airport, I was feeling melancholic. I was seeing the Bay as though for the first time. The blue of the sky was crisp and undiluted; the sloshing of the water against the rocks was sharper than usual. No one came to say farewell, but I was glad to have these last few moments to myself. I met the plane near the runway and held onto the cold steel rail to climb aboard. Before I knew it, I was looking back at the Blue Pearl from high in space, and marveling at modern interplanetary transportation.

Finally arriving, I examined my new home. It was a small stucco house with a tall ceiling in the living room. I still wasn't sure if I would like it there; after all, it was a lonely place and so far away from the familiar. I walked through the house, noticing the tiled floors and skylights in the ceiling of the cozy living room. When I came to the back porch, I stepped outside and took a walk to the marketplace to explore this "space station in outer space." The house was a short walk to the Monumento de la Revolución, and Pepita's.

Coming back, I encountered Judy, my roommate. Judy was a published writer who commuted frequently from this station to the Bay Area. We began discussing how we would decorate the house. Suddenly, the house started shaking and spinning out of control.

"Oh, God, this is it. This is the end," I said to her. The palms of my hands began to sweat, and my face froze with fear of impending death.

Judy's face, too, had that mark of terror where one's eyes are locked, staring into space. We waited for the crash. It seemed the house vibrated for an interminable length of time. Then, my consciousness struck through the fear. It was as though the shaking and spinning were purging out old thought patterns and cleansing my perceptions down to a cellular level. I almost expected to see a pile of rubble around my feet as evidence of the shakedown. I began to enjoy the sensations.

"Hang on—this means power!" I said to her, breaking through the trance.

The surging sensations continued. When the spinning stopped, I felt disappointed that I had not taken advantage of the opportunity to become enlightened. I walked to the front door and opened it to get another view of my location.

There lay the volcano, *"La Mujer Dormida,"* or, "The Sleeping Woman," the one who watches over us and reminds us to dream, and to remember.

As though talking to a friend, I said to myself, "Ah, yes, the Siksika of Alberta have a saying that if they can see the peaks of Natoyuyistico from wherever they stand, they must be home."

The tree-lined thoroughfares I was seeing weren't just anywhere; I was hearing the chiming of old church bells. I walked down the *Avenida de Los Muertos*, the Avenue of the Dead; climbed *La Pirámide del Sol*, the Pyramid of the Sun; felt the earth of my ancestors; tasted their *mole* and *chile verde*; and I heard their music and their laughter. I retraced my steps to the places I had visited in my youth—*La Catedral, La Alameda*.

When I came to *La Basílica* and saw *La Virgen de Guadalupe* face-to-face, I put the camera up to my eyes, but upon my heart, I felt the softness of her hand like a rose petal, cool and smooth.

"Sí, Madre, aquí estoy—Yes, Mother, I am here," I whispered to her as I lowered the camera. I was thinking in Spanish again.

When the Sun rose the following morning, I realized that if I could see *La Mujer Dormida, Ixtaccihuatl,* and the volcano that stands next to her, *Popocatepetl,* from wherever I stood, then, I must be home.

Endnotes

1. Highly recommended reading: Gunn Allen. *Grandmothers of the Light: A Medicine Woman's Sourcebook,* for a comprehensive discussion of the role of goddesses in the creation of life. Gunn Allen says that Tonantzin, the goddess believed to be Virgen de Guadalupe, is a more recent aspect of the early goddesses, and that she is akin to Thinking Woman, Selu, and Sky Woman, Spider Woman, and others._

2. León-Portilla. *Native Mesoamerican Spirituality: Ancient Myths, Discourses, Stories, Doctrines, Hymns, Poems from the Aztec, Yucatec, Quiche-Maya and Other Sacred Traditions* Tedlock trans., *Popol Vuh: The Mayan Book of the Dawn of Life.*

3. León-Portilla. *Native Mesoamerican Spirituality.*

4. Castaneda. *The Eagle's Gift.*

5. Le Clézio. *The Mexican Dream: Or, the Interrupted Thought of Amerindian Civilizations* Nicholson, *Mexican and American Mythology.*

6. León-Portilla. *Time and Reality in the Thought of the Maya.*

7. León-Portilla. *Time and Reality* Nicholson. *Mexican and American Mythology.*

8. Irwin. *The Dream Seekers: Native American Visionary Traditions of the Great Plains.*

9. Waters. *Mexico Mystique: The Coming Sixth World of Consciousness.*

10. León-Portilla. *Native Mesoamerican Spirituality* Tedlock, trans., *Popol Vuh.*

11. At the time of the Spanish Conquest in the early 1500s, many aspects of the culture were destroyed with the destruction of temples and burning of

books; but as León-Portilla points out *(Aztec Thought and Culture: A Study of the Ancient Nahuatl Mind; Time and Reality in the Thought of the Maya; Native Mesoamerican Spirituality: Ancient Myths, Discourses, Stories, Doctrines, Hymns, Poems from the Aztec, Yucatec, Quiche-Maya and Other Sacred Traditions; The Broken Spears: The Aztec Account of the Conquest of Mexico)*, history is written by the victors. For 460 years, the history of the conquest of Mexico was written from the perspective of the Spaniards. Traditionalist writers would have us believe that the Aztecs were defeated by a handful of Spaniards and that they had conquered not only the military and political, but also the spiritual, linguistic, and cultural aspects of Mesoamerican civilization. But as Tedlock, trans., *Popol Vuh*, further points out, dreamers took active steps to preserve the wisdom and practices of the Nahuatl culture, "… three lordly lineages that had once ruled the Quiche kingdom: the Cauecs, the Greathouses, the Lord Quiches. They worked in the middle of the sixteenth century." What concerned the authors of the new version of the *Popol Vuh* was to preserve the story that lay behind the ruins (pp. 25, 27). By allowing their young to enter into the monasteries, the nobility were establishing a link between the old and restructuring of a new religion. The "vanquished" anticipated and planned perpetuation of the culture and religion by their involvement in the remaking of the old religions and preservation of their history. *The Chilam Balam* and *The Popul Vuh*, sacred texts scattered throughout Europe, remained out of view of scholars until the late 1950s, when they began translations of them.

12. Bernal & Flores-Ortiz. *Latino Families: Sociohistorical Perspectives and Cultural Issues.*

13. Tedlock. *Dreaming*

14. A title given to a master Tibetan teacher; the word means *precious jewel.*

15. Jung. *Man and His Symbols.*

16. Barrón Druckrey. *The Contemporary Role of the Chicana Dreamer.*

17. Anonymous. *A Course in Miracles.*

18. www.chicanadreamer.com.

19. Gunn Allen. *Grandmothers of the Light: A Medicine Woman's Sourcebook.*

20. Nicholson. *Mexican and Central American Mythology.*

21. León-Portilla. *Time and Reality in the Thought of the Maya*

22. Tedlock, Trans. *Popol Vue: The Mayan Book of the Dawn of Life*

23. Nicholson. *Mexican and Central American Mythology.*

24. Gunn Allen. *Grandmothers of the Light: A Medicine Woman's Sourcebook.*

25. Nicholson. *Mexican and Central American Mythology*

26. León-Portilla, Ed. *Native Mesoamerican Spirituality: Ancient Myths, Discourses, Stories, Doctrines, Hymns, Poems from the Aztec, Yucatec, Quiche-Maya and Other Sacred Traditions*

27. León-Portilla. *Time and Reality.*

28. Ibid.

29. Castillo, Ed. *Goddess of the Americas: La Diosa de las Américas.*

30. Gunn Allen. *Grandmothers of the Light.*

31. Nicholson. *Mexican and Central American Mythology, 27.*

32. Ibid.

33. León-Portilla, Ed. *Native Mesoamerican Spirituality.*

34. Castaneda, *The Eagle's Gift*

35. Nicholson, *Mexican and Central American Mythology*

36. Nicholson. *Mexican and Central American Mythology, 15.*

37. León-Portilla, Ed. *Native Mesoamerican Spirituality: Ancient Myths, Discourses, Stories, Doctrines,*

    Hymns, Poems from the Aztec, Yucatec, Quiche-Maya and Other Sacred Traditions;

    Roys, Ed. and Trans. *Ritual of The Bacabs: A Book of Maya Incantations.*

38. Nicholson. *Mexican and Central American Mythology;* de la Coruña. *The Chronicles of Michoacán.*

39. León-Portilla. *Aztec Thought and Culture: A Study of the Ancient Nahuatl Mind.*

40. Castillo. *Massacre of the Dreamers: Essays on Xicanisma.*

41. León-Portilla. *Aztec Thought and Culture;* León-Portilla, Ed. *Native Mesoamerican Spirituality.*

42. Ibid.

43. Irwin. *The Dream Seekers: Native American Visionary Traditions of the Great Plains.*

44. León-Portilla. *Time and Reality in the Thought of the Maya,* 62-63;

    Roys, Ed. and Trans. *Ritual of The Bacabs: A Book of Maya Incantations.* According to Roys, this particular incantation was for healing breath passageways of a patient. When the shaman called on Crocodile, he was directing the cosmic forces to assist in the healing of the patient.

45. Irwin. *The Dream Seekers.*

46. Castaneda. *The Art of Dreaming,* 79.

47. de la Coruña. *The Chronicles of Michoacán;*

    Clezio. *The Mexican Dream: Or, the Interrupted Thought of Amerindian Civilizations.*

48. de la Coruña. *The Chronicles of Michoacán.*

49. Irwin. *The Dream Seekers.*

50. Castaneda. *The Art of Dreaming.*

51. Ibid, 7.

52. Irwin. *The Dream Seekers: Native American Visionary Traditions of the Great Plains.*

53. Fletcher and La Flesche, as cited in Irwin, *The Dream Seekers,* 128.

54. Castaneda. *The Art of Dreaming.*

55. Tedlock, Trans. *Popol Vuh: The Mayan Book of the Dawn of Life;*

    León-Portilla. *Aztec Thought and Culture;*

    León-Portilla. *Time and Reality.*

56. Ibid.

57. Ibid.

58. Waters. *Mexico Mystique: The Coming Sixth World of Consciousness.*

59. *Anzaldúa. Borderlands—La Frontera: The New Mestiza; Castillo. Massacre of the Dreamers; Castillo, Ed. Goddess of the Americas—La Diosa de las Américas; Gunn Allen. The Sacred Hoop: Recovering the Feminine in Ameri-*

can Indian Traditions;Gunn Allen. Grandmothers of the Light: A Medicine Woman's Sourcebook; Rebolledo. Women Singing in the Snow: A Cultural Analysis of Chicana Literature; and others too numerous to list.

60. de la Coruña. *The Chronicles of Michoacán.*

61. Narby, J., *The Cosmic Serpent: DNA And The Origins of Knowledge*

62. Tarthang Tulku, The Nyingma Institute in Berkeley, California has several books published by Dharma Publishing on Kum Nye Relaxation.

63. Published by the Foundation for Inner Peace http://www.acim.org/

64. www.attitudinalhealing.org/

65. *Roberts, J., Personal Reality*

66. Bernal and Flores-Ortiz. *Latino Families: Sociohistorical Perspectives and Cultural Issues.*

67. de la Coruña. *The Chronicles of Michoacán.*

68. Ibid., 205.

69. Ibid.

70. Castillo, *Goddess of the Americas*

71. León-Portilla, Ed. *Native Mesoamerican Spirituality: Ancient Myths, Discourses, Stories, Doctrines, Hymns, Poems from the Aztec, Yucatec, Quiche-Maya and Other Sacred Traditions*, 202.

72. Castaneda. *Second Ring of Power*, 274, a977.

73. Gunn Allen. *Grandmothers of the Light.*

74. Irving, *The Dream Seekers: Native Americcan Visionary Traditions of the Great Plains.*

75. Gunn Allen. *Grandmothers of the Light: A Medicine Woman's Sourcebook.*

76. Irwin. *The Dream Seekers: Native American Visionary Traditions of the Great Plains.*

77. Ibid.

78. Tedlock, Ed. *Dreaming: Anthropological and Psychological Interpretations.*

79. Tedlock, trans. *Popol Vuh.*

80. León-Portilla. *Aztec Thought and Culture: A Study of the Nahuatl Mind.*

81. Fletcher and La Flesche as cited in Irwin, 128.

82. Irwin. *The Dream Seekers: Native American Visionary Traditions of the Great Plains.*

83. Neihardt. *Black Elk Speaks*

84. Nicholson. *Mexican and American Mythology.*

85. Castaneda. *The Eagle's Gift*

86. Leon-Portilla, Ed. *Native Mesoamerican Spirituality: Ancient Myths, Discourses, Stories, Doctrines, Hymns, and Poems from the Aztec, Yucatec, Quiche-Maya and other Sacred Traditions,* 101.

87. Ibid.

88. Gill & Sullivan. *Native American Mythology.*

89. Gunn Allen. *The Sacred Hoop: Recovering the Feminine in American Indian Traditions.*

90. Leon-Portilla. Davis, trans. *Aztec Thought and Culture: A study of the Ancient Nahuatl Mind.*

91. Ibid.

92. Flores-Ortiz. *Theorizing Justice in Chicano Families.* In Flores and Carey, Eds. *Family Therapy with Hispanics: Toward Appreciating Diversity.*

93. Anzaldua, G., *Borderlands: La Frontera, the New Mestiza*

94. California Foundation for Inner Peace. *A Course in Miracles*

95. Whenever I started whining as a child, my mother threatened that if I didn't stop, the coyote would come for me. El Coyote was similar to the Bogey Man.

96. Pinkola Estes. *Women Who Run With The Wolves*

97. Irwin. *The Dream Seekers: Native American Visionary traditions of the Great Plains.*

98. Gill & Sullivan. *Dictionary of Native American Mythology.*

99. Castaneda. *The Eagle's Gift.*

100. Gunn Allen. *Grandmothers of the Light*

101. Gunn Allen. *Grandmothers of the Light*

References

Anonymous. (1975). *A Course in Miracles*. Glen Ellen CA: Foundation for Inner Peace.

Anzaldúa, G. (1999). *Borderlands La frontera: The New Mestiza* (2nd ed.). San Francisco: Aunt Lute Books.

Barrón Druckrey, E. (2001). *The Contemporary Role of the Chicana Dreamer*. Tiburon: PhD dissertation.

Bernal, G., & Flores-Ortiz, Y. (1984). *Latino families: Sociohistorical Perspectives and Cultural Issues*. Nueva Epoca, 1(1), 4-8.

Castaneda, C. (1968). *The Teachings of Don Juan: A Yaqui Way of Knowledge*. New York: Ballantine Books.

Castaneda, C. (1972). *Journey to Ixtlan: The Lessons of Don Juan*. New York: Simon & Schuster.

Castaneda, C. (1974). *Tales of Power*. New York: Simon & Schuster.

Castaneda, C. (1977). *The Second Ring of Power*. New York: Simon & Schuster.

Castaneda, C. (1981). *The Eagle's Gift*. New York: Simon & Schuster.

Castaneda, C. (1993). *The Art of Dreaming*. New York: HarperCollins.

Castillo, A. (1994). *Massacre of the Dreamers: Essays on Xicanisma*. New York: Penguin Books.

Castillo, A. (Ed.). (1996). *Goddess of the Americas La diosa de las Américas*. New York: Riverhead Books.

de la Coruña, Martín de Jesús. (1970). *The Chronicles of Michoacán* (E. R. Craine & R. C. Reindorp, Eds. and Trans.). Norman, OK: The University of Oklahoma Press. (Original work published in 1541).

Flores-Ortiz, Y. G. (in press). "Re/membering the Body: Latina Testimonies of Social and Family Violence." In A. J. Aldama (Ed.), *Violence and the Body* [no pp yet]. Davis, CA: University of California.

Gill, S. D. & Sullivan, I. F. (1992). *Dictionary of Native American Mythology*. New York: Oxford University Press.

Gunn Allen, P. (1986). *The Sacred Hoop: Recovering the Feminine in American Indian Traditions*. Boston: Beacon Press.

Gunn Allen, P. (1991). *Grandmothers of the Light: A Medicine Woman's Sourcebook*. Boston: Beacon Press.

Irwin, L. (1994). *The Dream Seekers: Native American Visionary Traditions of the Great Plains*. Norman, OK: University of Oklahoma Press.

Jung, C. G. & von Franz, M.-L. (Eds.). (1964). *Man and His Symbols*. Garden City, New York: Doubleday & Company. [The second editor took over after Jung died.]

Le Clézio, J.-M. G. (1993). *The Mexican Dream: Or, The Interrupted Thought of Amerindian Civilizations* (T. L. Fagan, Trans.). Chicago: The University of Chicago Press. (Original work published 1988).

León-Portilla, M. (1963). *Aztec Thought and Culture: A Study of the Ancient Nahuatl Mind*. (J. E. Davis, Trans.). Norman, OK: The University of Oklahoma Press. (Original work published 1956).

León-Portilla, M. (1973). *Time and Reality in the Thought of the Maya*. (C. L. Boilès & F. Horcasitas, Trans.). Boston: Beacon Press. (Original work published 1968).

León-Portilla, M. (Ed.). (1980). *Native Mesoamerican Spirituality: Ancient Myths, Discourses, Stories, Doctrines, Hymns, Poems from the Aztec, Yucatec,*

Quiche-Maya and Other Sacred Traditions. (M. León-Portilla, J. O. A. Anderson, CE Dibble & M. S. Edmonson, Trans.). Mahwah, New Jersey: Paulist Press.

León-Portilla, M. (Ed.). (1992). *The Broken Spears: The Aztec Account of the Conquest of Mexico*. (Rev. ed.). (L. Kemp, Trans.). Boston: Beacon Press. (Original work published 1959) ["expanded and updated ed." per front cover].

Merrill, W. (1992). "The Rarámuri Stereotype of Dreams." In B. Tedlock (Ed.), *Dreaming: Anthropological and psychological interpretations* (pp. 194-219). Santa Fe, NM: School of American Research Press.

Nicholson, I. (1967) *Mexican and Central American Mythology*. London: Paul Hamlyn Limited.

(1996). *Popol Vuh: The Mayan Book of the Dawn of Life* (Rev. ed.). (D. Tedlock, trans.). New York: Simon & Schuster. [Translated from the Quiché].

Rebolledo, T. D. (1995). *Women Singing in the Snow: A Cultural Analysis of Chicana Literature*. Tucson, AZ: The University of Arizona Press.

Roberts, J. (1972). *Seth Speaks*. New York, NY, Bantam Books.

Roys, R. L. (Ed. and Trans.). (1965). *Ritual of the Bacabs: A Book of Maya Incantations*. Norman, OK: University of Oklahoma Press.

Shulman, D., & Stroumsa, G. G. (Eds.). (1999). *Dream Cultures: Explorations in the Comparative History of Dreaming*. New York: Oxford University Press.

Smith, B.. (1968). *Mexico: A History in Art*.

Tedlock, B. (Ed.). (1992). *Dreaming: Anthropological and Psychological Interpretations*. Santa Fe, NM: School of American Research Press.

Trotter II, R. T., & Chavira, J. A. (1997). *Curanderismo: Mexican American Folk Healing*. (2nd ed.). Athens, GA: The University of Georgia Press.

Waters, F. (1975). *Mexico Mystique: The Coming Sixth World of Consciousness*. Chicago: The Swallow Press.

Index

Artists xvi, xxi, 12, 15, 25, 48, 61, 125

Assemblage Point 29, 111, 119

Attention xiii, xxii, xxvi, 7, 8, 9, 27, 35, 40, 41, 43, 44, 49, 51, 55, 56, 61, 62, 64, 65, 68, 84, 85, 89, 90, 103, 106, 109, 115, 116, 119, 120, 121, 123

Attitudinal Healing 6, 39, 52, 54, 73, 97, 102, 103

Autogenic training 6, 38, 52, 85, 118

Black Elk xxvii, 71, 79

Center for Attitudinal
    Healing xxiv, 6, 19, 26, 37, 39, 52, 54, 61, 68, 70, 71, 72, 73, 80, 87, 94, 97, 102, 103, 121, 126, 143

Chronicles of Michoacan 49

Coatlicue 18, 122

Course in Miracles 13, 38, 39, 97, 108, 141

Creation Stories xxiii, xxvi, xxvii, 17, 18, 20, 60, 71, 86, 87, 111, 113, 125

Daykeepers 3, 72

Death xxvii, 2, 16, 18, 19, 22, 30, 31, 39, 45, 50, 58, 60, 68, 70, 71, 73, 74, 76, 77, 78, 83, 101, 102, 103, 105, 123, 132

Death shows
    compassion 3, 14, 18, 30, 53, 56, 65, 73, 75, 90, 92, 100, 101, 106, 116, 122

Destiny xvii, xviii, xxi, xxiii, xxvi, xxvii, xxviii, 2, 4, 25, 26, 33, 49, 55, 56, 58, 60, 61, 63, 66, 67, 68, 69, 70, 71, 72, 74, 80, 83, 84, 87, 92, 94, 100, 103, 110, 112, 119, 125, 126, 128

Dream Awareness 4, 8, 35, 63, 65, 73

Dream Map xviii, xxi, xxii, xxiii, xxv, xxviii, 3, 9, 11, 12, 24, 26, 35, 80, 109, 110, 111, 121, 127, 128, 129

Dream yoga 6, 37, 38

Eagle 29, 30, 107, 120, 121, 141

East 18, 19, 27, 28, 37, 101, 102, 122, 123, 128

El Destino 60, 67

Elders xvi, xviii, xxii, 42, 43, 66, 67, 125

Flying xxi, 41, 42, 43, 55, 89

Gifts of Power xxiii, 69, 83, 111, 124, 128

God of Duality xxiii, xxiv, xxv, 17, 18, 19, 22, 26, 60, 86, 87, 91, 104

Grandmother xvi, xviii, xxi, xxvi, 1, 6, 8, 12, 16, 17, 34, 50, 51, 52, 53, 54, 55, 56, 63, 68, 79, 98, 114, 115, 116, 122, 123

La Virgen de Guadalupe xxiii, xxv, 18, 21, 51, 109, 116, 122, 133

Mayan Dreamers 3

Medicine women xxi, 48, 99, 105, 126

Mestizo xxv

Metamorphosis 21, 71, 119, 120

Moctezuma 25, 26

Mother Cedar 30, 72

Mystics xxi, xxiii, 15, 48, 94, 125, 128

Nagualismo xxiv, xxv, xxvi, 20, 21, 22, 29, 32, 86, 87, 111, 118, 119, 120, 123

Nature xiii, xxiv, xxvii, 1, 15, 18, 21, 27, 32, 34, 35, 37, 44, 56, 61, 64, 80, 82, 83, 84, 85, 86, 87, 88, 89, 90, 91, 92, 96, 105, 118, 119, 120, 121, 123, 127

North xviii, xxii, xxiii, xxvi, 18, 27, 28, 30, 83, 101, 102, 103, 120, 122, 123, 128

Nyingma Institute xiv, 6, 11, 31, 38, 39, 51, 53, 54, 97

Old Dreamers xxi, xxii, xxiv, xxvi, xxvii, xxviii, 13, 22, 25, 27, 29, 31, 32, 33, 35, 44, 48, 83, 86, 87, 93, 104, 105, 106, 109, 110, 111, 113, 114, 119, 122, 123, 127

Ometeotl xxiii

Popol Vuh xxv, 18, 60, 143

Psychological
    homelessness xxvii, xxviii, 3, 94, 99, 101, 103, 105, 110, 125

Quetzalcoatl 18, 20, 21, 22, 109, 111, 113, 121

Red and Black Ink xxv, 26, 71, 73, 86

Roaming Chief 30, 72

Sacred Gifts xxi, xxvi, xxvii, 33, 36, 61, 70, 71, 78, 127, 129

Sages xxiii, xxiv, xxvi, 23, 26, 29

Shape shifting 127

South 27, 28, 48, 55, 102, 103, 112, 122, 123, 128

Spanish Conquest xxiv, 25, 30, 32

Spirit Beings xvi, xxii, xxiv, xxvi, 8, 28, 29, 30, 32, 33, 35, 43, 44, 47, 49, 56, 67, 69, 119, 121

Spiritual Discipline 6, 13

The Four Directions xiii, xiv, 18, 32, 83, 119, 128

The Quadrant 102

Time and Space xxv, xxvi, 18, 20, 21, 22, 27, 29, 35, 54, 55, 83, 87, 102, 104, 111, 113, 114, 117, 122, 123

Tlaloc God of Rain 83

Tlalocan 101, 108, 110

Tlamitamines xxiii, xxiv, xxvi, 25, 26, 30, 31, 33, 68, 93, 109

Tonantzin xxiii

Transformation xxii, xxv, xxvi, xxvii, 4, 10, 12, 17, 20, 22, 24, 25, 26, 30, 32, 33, 35, 44, 49, 57, 61, 69, 87, 89, 93, 94, 105, 106, 109, 110, 111, 113, 116, 118, 119, 120, 121, 123, 128, 129

West 18, 19, 27, 28, 101, 102, 103, 122, 123, 128

Worldview xvii, xxii, xxiii, xxv, 26, 32, 48, 54, 83, 86, 94, 105, 115

Xpiyacoc xxiii, 18

Year 2011 c.e. xxiv

978-0-595-46343-5
0-595-46343-6

www.ingramcontent.com/pod-product-compliance
Lightning Source LLC
Chambersburg PA
CBHW020419290526
45785CB00002B/643